Nobody nicked 'em

How we started a toy library
in the East End of London

by Joanna Grana
assisted by Jonathan Masters

Published by the Calouste Gulbenkian Foundation
UK Branch, London, 1983.

To Alvaro, who gave me the space;
to Marg Behrman and Richard Mills,
who gave us 'lift-off'; and to all the
parents who provided the power to
fuel the project, without whom the
Toy Library would not have existed.

Joanna Grana

Further copies
are available from the
Calouste Gulbenkian Foundation

© 1983 Calouste Gulbenkian Foundation
98 Portland Place
London W1N 4ET
Telephone 01-636 5313/7

ISBN 0 903319 34 9
Photographs by Chris Schwarz   Tel: (01) 263 6761
Cover design by John Minnion   Tel: (01) 341 3308
Produced by PPR Printing London W1   Tel: (01) 437 1430

CONTENTS

FOREWORD

It was apparent at the time Joanna Grana's refreshingly direct application was received four years ago that the story of the project would be worth retailing for the benefit of others, and that the applicant was the person to write it. The book would bring out the project's distinctive features as an important experiment in the provision of facilities for the pre-school child in a highly deprived multiracial area. It would highlight the willingness of a group of local mothers with young children to accept responsibility for the project; their professional understanding of the educational use of toys; and their awareness of the special needs of isolated Asian mothers and their children.

The book, as we now have it, does all this and more. It is divided into two parts. The first part is a chronological account of the project as it developed. The second details four major aspects of the practical business of launching and running the Library. There are also two useful appendices.

Much of the book's value resides in its 'warts and all' approach. Mistakes are not glossed over; equally with achievements and successes, they are recounted not for their own sake but as experiences from which the organisers have learnt and from which others may benefit. Similarly, they acknowledge their debt to others whom they had the wisdom to consult—people like local community workers and those involved in neighbouring toy libraries and the Toy Libraries Association.

Not the least valuable feature of the book is the modesty and candour with which the tale is told, as is movingly exemplified in the following quotation: 'There have been disappointments too, when for instance our trust had been abused and a toy not returned, or the occasions when we had failed to pick up someone's need for support and decipher it in time. These all contributed to our process of learning'.

The Foundation would like to thank all who have been concerned in the production of this book, above all the author, Joanna Grana, and Jonathan Masters who assisted her with the writing.

Richard Mills
UK Branch
Calouste Gulbenkian Foundation

INTRODUCTION

Burdett Toy Library was brought into being by a group of ordinary people. By describing our experiences I hope that other ordinary people can identify with us—and perhaps try something similar themselves.

When we began we had little in common other than the fact of our loneliness. Recognising that we wanted to meet other parents with young children made us aware of the same need in our neighbours. This primed our collective enthusiasm for making the Toy Library work. We had no money, no experience, just an empty front room in an old house and a feeling that if we tried hard enough we could change things.

The house was in the East End of London, conventionally described as a multi-cultural urban deprived area. The details included here reflect that and are by-products of our particular development. They are neither intended to be a blue-print nor comprehensive, since each project has its own character and direction. Ours is still changing, reflecting the interests of those currently involved with its running. Rather than a hand-book for the self-help movement, the intention has been to describe, at a personal level, what were to us very real struggles and the unexpected benefits we reaped.

With the hindsight of experience we can recognise that there were political implications to what we attempted, highlighted by subsequent expenditure cuts which have strongly affected Under-Fives' provision and increased the interest in voluntary projects. But for us at the time, there were no politics; the excitement of the venture carried us along.

Our enterprise turned out to be a Toy Library aimed at alleviating isolation in homebound parents of children under five. It might well have taken one of a dozen routes. To make the process simpler for anyone wishing to follow a path similar to ours, I have suggested a few signposts in Appendix 1.

PART ONE
The project's development

1 How it all began

What we were aiming for: the toy library today

It was Christmas 1977 when I and my husband, Alvaro, together with our daughter Natalia who was then seven months old, moved into a community house owned by the Bow Mission, along with three other newcomers. We had heard about it by chance—an experiment to see whether the occupants of the house could make part of it, and themselves, available to the local community. There were no rules about the form this should take and we were complete beginners. Our next door neighbours, however, had lived in the area for several years and were already involved in the local community, partly through projects such as Adult Literacy classes, partly as foster parents.

Alvaro had found a job as a Playgroup Leader nearby and the others in the house either worked or studied during the day. It was unsettling to be at home all day in a place in which I did not feel 'at home' at all, since I knew hardly anyone or anything in the area. One afternoon I ventured close enough to what I had assumed was a nursery to discover that it was actually a One O'Clock Club open to anyone with a child under five. I was delighted to find that Natalia would be able to mix with the other children and try out the toys and equipment while, at last, I could meet other parents.

It was not quite so easy! My accent, clothes, and probably my manner, seemed to be a barrier to my being accepted. I could talk to the staff or the children but the mothers—chatting in their literally closed circle of chairs—made no effort to welcome a stranger to their group. Natalia obviously enjoyed going, however, so I went quite frequently and in so doing learnt a little about the local customs. Over the months I began to recognise the other 'outsiders' and we gradually made friends. At times I felt inclined to cross the grass and invite a new mother who was sitting alone to join us, but I soon realised that this did not work. Most preferred to sit tight although solitary—suspicious of this unsolicited friendliness.

Another way for local mothers to meet and exchange a few words, rather than merely pass on the 'shopping beat', was at the local clinic. On Thursdays those with babies and toddlers would congregate for weighing, jabs and so on. However, conversations were often cut short when the doctor called for one of us. There were some who seemed eager but too shy even to risk this encounter, and some whose wariness of strangers blocked any contact at all. These included the Asian women, often attending in groups of two or three as if for support. The staff frequently had a hard job trying to communicate beyond the basic 'name and age' queries, and I saw signs among other mothers present not of sympathy but very often of annoyance and even derision. These quiet fearful women, I later discovered, were mainly from the rural areas of Bangladesh: little-educated and simple people who must have found city life and British customs in particular quite mystifying and even threatening. The barriers of culture and language were much higher than any I had ever experienced. It caused me to wonder if there could be some way of forming a bridge so that our common experience of motherhood might serve as a base for future communication.

It was against this background that we began to think about ways of bringing families from a variety of backgrounds together in an open and welcoming environment. The idea of starting a Toy Library, when we hit on it, seemed to appeal at several levels. First, it seemed well-tailored to the needs of the area, full of hard-up families whom we felt sure would enjoy borrowing toys. Second, it appealed to those of us who would be responsible for its running. I had come to realise that my input would have to fit around caring for Natalia, while both Alvaro and I favoured our vacant 'community' front room being used by young children since our interest and experience lay in that field. Third, it seemed a flexible enough scheme to allow developments in a variety of directions, for example, enabling parents to offer mutual help such as language classes or babysitting. Something in our favour which we only realised later was that, being opposite the clinic, we were conveniently close for an existing group of parents who not only had practical difficulties in travelling far with young children, but often felt bound by strong cultural traditions, to stay within their 'patch'. Bearing these factors in mind we realised that friendships made at the Toy Library would be more likely to flourish among those who lived relatively near each other, and that these meetings could indirectly enhance their feeling of belonging to a real community—something our area definitely lacked.

The author with some co-founders

2 Getting our bearings

Having decided on a Toy Library as a possible use for our front room, we kept our eyes and ears open for information on what to do next. Our next door neighbours pointed us in the direction of Newham Parents' Centre which was having an open day. Although on that visit we felt very much like country cousins, the people we met were friendly and reassuring about our tentative plans and we saw for ourselves that even such well-established and flourishing schemes as theirs could start from small beginnings. Something about the place gave us the confidence to attempt a similar venture.

They suggested we make contact with a nearby organisation called Community Links which, among other projects, ran a toy library. In those days, going twice to Newham seemed quite an adventure, but by now we were hot on the trail and eager to continue. Alvaro even took the day off work to meet them. We bought a hard-backed notebook to record our impressions and useful information, a symbol of the jelling of our dreams into something solid.

They opened our eyes to the various tasks we were going to be faced with: registering as a charity, opening a bank account, applying for grants, fund-raising, printing leaflets, publicity, equipping the Toy Library and finding a friendly accountant and solicitor to turn to for advice. They wisely stressed the importance of making local contacts first and involving them in choosing and structuring the project's activities rather than a group of us deciding things in advance. Equally important, they told us of the existence of the Toy Libraries Association and two of their publications called *How to start a Toy Library* and *The ABC of Toys* (see Appendix 2 (2)). The address seemed like part of a fairy story, but did in fact lead to our receiving a wallet of information covering all the questions one would expect from a would-be Toy Library.

Once I had digested this material I came to the conclusion that to start with my time would be well spent in getting to know the existing facilities of our local community (so as to know whom to contact for support later on) and secondly in visiting a variety of toy libraries to learn how they worked. It was one thing to realise that I had time to do this research, but another to know how to go about it. Fortunately a friendly health visitor lent me her list of papers containing addresses of clinics, schools, Social Services offices, Citizens Advice Bureaux and so on. I copied it all down—even though nine-tenths of the places were unknown to me. This 'homework' proved invaluable, greatly lessening the disadvantage I felt in being a newcomer to the area, and helping me to get my 'community bearings'. We often referred to that list later on when other parents visiting the Toy Library needed specific information about provision, particularly concerning under-fives.

Meanwhile I visited a number of toy libraries in our area, alone at first and later with the others who became involved with setting up our Toy Library. The information pack from the Toy Libraries Association contained names and addresses of all known toy libraries as well as potential toy libraries in each part of the country. The first one I contacted was nearby in Whitechapel, Sunley House, which catered for families with handicapped children. I was warmly welcomed and given a great deal of useful information (see Part II Section 1). Two pieces of advice stand out in my mind: first, that it would take at least six months to get fully operational—which at the time seemed over-cautious; and second, as I discovered in time, that once involved in a toy library it can take over one's life!

Next I visited St Margaret's Toy Library in Bethnal Green. It was just getting off the ground and had modelled itself on Sunley House. At its opening I met local social workers, health visitors and a liaison worker with the local ESN school, part of whose jobs it would be to refer particular families to the Toy Library. This gave me some insight into ways of linking up with local professionals.

My third visit was to a toy library on our doorstep based in the offices of the Social Services in Bow. It was funded by the Borough to cater for child-minders and playgroups. Apart from lending toys it also supplied equipment such as cots, playpens and sterilising equipment on a temporary basis. Perhaps the main lesson I learned there was the importance of making contact with the right person; the social workers involved with running it were not available and my visit was largely wasted. I realised that I should have been less concerned with offending an individual's pride and more emphatic when making the appointment, stressing that it must be with the person I really wanted to consult.

On finding so many toy libraries in our area I became a bit disillusioned and wondered whether our venture would be totally superfluous. On reflection I realised that they served different populations. Our aim was to be a *community* toy library open to families with young children in our immediate area for whom similar services were either unavailable or too difficult to reach.

Most users live within walking distance of the toy library

3 For the good of the community?

About this time we began to consider how we were going to find enough money to get the project off the ground. Our expertise and confidence in fund-raising were nil. This, coupled with our lack of anything concrete to show to any organisation which might consider financing us, makes it seem in retrospect quite remarkable that we ever broke out of this chicken-and-egg situation. A crucial ingredient of our success was undoubtedly our consultation with people highly experienced at approaching grant-giving bodies—in our case the Bow Mission, and in particular the Rev David Moore. We asked his advice over our first attempt at approaching a charitable foundation.

By chance I had read about a scheme for the inner cities which seemed to be geared to projects similar to ours where the people living in an area set up something to help themselves. We put together a letter introducing ourselves to the grant-giving organisation. Although the letter was already in its envelope, it was never sent because once I had shown a copy to David Moore I saw that it was poorly written on several counts. In fact that meeting held primarily to discuss the wording of the application caused us to pause and re-think the purpose of the whole venture.

I summarised the advice he gave at the meeting:
1. The project should not just be the work of one person/group, but involve the local community.
2. Essential to research into who and what the local community actually comprises—how many Asians, what other facilities already exist which cater for such groups, cultural patterns regarding toys, importance of play, etc.
3. Work out exact financial needs—how money will be spent, provide proof that the project can administer funds properly (see also Part II Section 3).

This discussion took place three weeks after our first encounter in Newham which had so inspired us that we had felt 'the sky's the limit'. It brought us down to earth, caused us to alter our immediate goals considerably, and to approach the matter rather more scientifically. Apart from collecting far more information, we realised that an essential ingredient was not only telling the people of the area about the idea we had dreamed up, but actually *testing* whether it was appropriate and appealing enough for some of them to want to share in its creation. That seemed an incredibly daunting task and much more challenging than merely learning the mechanics of how to finance and organise the details of the project. Looking back, this was probably because I was so immersed in it that it felt as if *I could be rejected.*

Certain other aspects of our conversation disquieted me and shook the naive optimism which had brought me this far. It had never crossed my mind that there could be anything wrong in what we were aiming to do from the house. After all, if we were prepared to give our time and energy for the good of the community surely that was admirable? Some people, I learned, thought otherwise. How could people who were not truly part of the community come in and impose ideas and expect them to take root? How could we call ourselves East Enders or come anywhere near representing East End needs and wishes? To top it all, we had dampening discussions with our next door neighbour who had lived locally for a few years. He had a host of dismal tales to tell about projects that had failed time after time due to lack of local support. He also queried whether it was right for voluntary groups to try to fill gaps rather than to put pressure on the State to make better provision. I respected his greater experience and political knowledge but my innate pig-headedness forced me to say 'Well let's give it a try at least'.

Once we had resolved to carry on it was comforting to know that we could rely on David Moore for moral support and practical information. Having an ally at this stage took a load off my mind, rather like having a navigator through unknown waters. We discovered, for example, that for the time being we could have charitable status for the house as a unit under the wing of the Bow Mission since they were both a charity and our landlords. He also told us that we could consult the local Law Centre for free advice on drawing up a constitution so as to become eventually a charity in our own right with aims of our own. Being a charity makes it easier to apply for money (see Part II Section 4). Another useful and time-saving piece of information was the address of a nearby centre where stencils could be cut electrically so that any design could be copied directly instead of us having to draw it on. This meant much better quality leaflets and posters.

4 The wheel begins to turn

We bought excellent toys at bargain prices

At that meeting with David Moore we realised that there was an art in applying for money and presenting one's case, and above all that a project needs to have people. So we set about trying to put flesh upon the bones. In fact we were returning to a point from which we should have started—the community.

My great stumbling block now was to know how to set about this. After several fruitless journeys and dead-ends spanning several weeks, I happened to pass the local Citizens Advice Bureau. I went in to see if they could help. By good fortune they were able to put me in touch with a Community Worker, Marg, based in the same building and whose job it was to help people in just my position. She turned out to be our salvation since not only could she advise and help us to make effective contact with the community, but, equally importantly, her enthusiasm was infectious at a time when despair was beginning to creep in.

We arranged a day for her to come to the house and over a cup of tea we planned our strategy. She suggested we contact the Tenants' Associations on nearby estates and a Pre-School Playgroup training course for local mothers (see Appendix 2 (3)) to sound out potentially interested people. There were also various groups and professionals to make contact with for advice and skills. One was a branch of the local Adult Education Institute which offered Asian translation of leaflets, others included the Educational Welfare Officer, the local Gingerbread group for one-parent families, and Sebastian, the Community Liaison Worker attached to the Social Services.

Marg suggested that we should try to stage an exhibition to interest local parents and to explain what we were hoping to do. It seemed that the clinic opposite the house would be the best place. After discussing this proposal with an experienced worker at Sunley House, we decided that toys themselves would make the best exhibits, backed up by people to talk about the proposed project.

At this time I had a response to the letter I had written to the Community Relations Council requesting information on the particular ethnic composition of our immediate area. The response was Fatima Parker who came to the house. She was optimistic that we might qualify for a grant from the Commission for Racial Equality (see Appendix 2 (8)) and advised us how to apply. However, she was not optimistic about involving mothers from ethnic minority groups and warned us that they were unlikely to feel confident enough to participate in the initial stages before the project was seen to be functioning.

Meanwhile there remained the basic question of inviting a broad cross-section of people to a preliminary meeting to discuss the possibility of starting a toy library. To help us on our way Marg had advised us to contact Sebastian, the Community Liaison Officer, so I made an appointment to see him. Although I remember feeling rather gauche when we first met—finding his professionalism a bit overpowering—he gave me a great deal of sound advice which I later summarised:

1. Try to avoid the project becoming one person's idea imposed by the leader on the rest.
2. Stress that the success of the toy library will depend on local interest and involvement.
3. Lay the onus on the local residents themselves and make certain you have a minimum level of involvement (say 20 people) before going on. The larger the initial group the less likely it is to discourage others from joining later on as the project gains strength.

As a professional community worker Sebastian obviously wanted to ensure that there was a real need for the toy library in the area and knew from experience that a slow broad-based approach was the ideal. Unfortunately I did not have his detachment and my instinct was to plunge in at the deep end rather than risk being numbed in the shallows. At the same time I was worried that unless there were some visible signs of achievement at the first meeting people might not be motivated to carry on. Sebastian on the other hand minimised the need for such incentives. His favourite theme was to stress that if there was no real interest by members of the community, the lack of true roots would mean that the project would fall by the wayside however enthusiastic we, the initiators, were. To us, starting from scratch seemed both challenging and frightening!

To begin to test the level of local interest I visited two groups of local mothers—one at a Mother and Toddlers Club and the other at the One O'Clock Club—to talk about the advantages of a toy library and to discover if they were interested in getting one going. The response seemed fairly positive, enough for us to arrange a meeting the following Monday morning when most people were free.

With great glee I returned to Sebastian who had mentioned at our last meeting that he would help me duplicate a poster for publicity. He immediately advised me to redraft the one I had brought. He suggested that it should contain much less written information and focus, for example, on a drawing of a child playing. Not having funds for printing I had been too keen to maximise this chance of free publicity and had crammed on far too much information. Sebastian assured me that we could do several leaflets later on—each covering a different topic. He showed me in detail both how to type the stencil and duplicate it correctly as I had never done this before. We printed 500 leaflets on bright orange paper.

Over the next three days a friend and I distributed the leaflets to local schools, One O'Clock Clubs, shops, passers-by with children and any families with children we met on the estates within a 10 minute radius. Most of the shop-keepers were happy to put up posters, even if slightly cynical. On the estates I felt a little uncomfortable, aware of being a newcomer suggesting something rather outlandish which I sensed was being received rather sceptically.

Although I was pleased to see our orange leaflets adorning so many windows, Gloria, the Health Visitor said gloomily 'nobody ever reads notices around here'. It was her experience that the local people, without the habit of reading for pleasure, tended to fight shy of the written word. She, for her part, was busy telling as many people as she could—those she felt might be interested or might enjoy the chance of being involved in a group of any kind because they were isolated.

At that time we had a stroke of good luck. A neighbour had been involved in a scheme run by a toy firm through which housewives, as its agents, could display toys at home and sell them to their friends. The firm having just changed its policy was now asking the agents to buy the stock and pay for the toys in advance. My neighbour felt I might be interested as they were offering these toys at greatly reduced prices. I speedily offered to take over her stock of toys and to act as their agent through the future Toy Library. They were very generous and interested in our plans allowing us to have £60.00

worth of toys for £25.00. The toys were of excellent quality and I began to feel that things were at last moving ahead.

Over the weekend we put the finishing touches to the community room where we were going to house the Toy Library. Alvaro had built shelves to display the toys we had acquired—our major tangible achievement to date. Now that we were approaching the moment of truth we started to get cold feet. I felt that the room would be seen as inadequate. It was not very big. The colours were a bit gloomy and it looked out onto waste land lined by a row of boarded up railway arches. The best thing was perhaps that the room's walls were completely blank so we could do just what we liked with them.

Going home from the toy library

5 Our first public meeting

It was Monday 22nd May the day of our first public meeting. I stuck a notice on the front door of our house showing children playing. It said, 'Yes the meeting is here today! Come on in!' Then I waited to see what would happen. Inside the toys were on display along with the catalogues and literature I had received from the Toy Libraries Association.

In the event our 500 leaflets did not seem to have much drawing power. Seven people turned up, including Marg, who made a point of introducing each new person to the others by name, helping to make them feel welcome. One person came as the result of a leaflet through her door—we had specifically leafleted her street as Gloria the Health Visitor thought she might be interested; another came from the local playgroup—sent over by Gloria with a tin of biscuits! Two others came from the Mother and Toddlers Club and One O'Clock Club, one lived around the corner and had seen a notice in the window, and the last one was an acquaintance of Marg! All the others with whom I had arranged the meeting—supposedly at a convenient time for them— didn't come. This taught me an important lesson about the subtleties of help volunteered but not forthcoming. For a while I found people who had said they would come avoiding my eye in the street. I had become a visible reminder of their bad conscience. It was hard to convey that I hadn't taken it personally and recognised they had every right to change their minds. I realised I needed to relax about involvement otherwise my anxiety could discourage potentially interested people. As Sebastian had taught me—if we pushed ahead too fast, forcing people into what they were either not suited to or not yet ready for, we would only get sickly growth from weak roots. I slowly began to appreciate this. Although a number of people dropped out over the coming weeks, there was a steadily deepening commitment among those to whom the project really appealed. In retrospect these 'stayers' were people who were not part of an established group such as a Mothers and Toddlers Club, consequently their commitment could be whole-hearted since it satisfied a need not met elsewhere.

But that was all in the future and this was our first meeting. One of those present, a strong feminist, came straight to the point and criticised the publicity poster for being addressed only to 'mums' and not parents in general. As time passed I began to appreciate how much fathers—who were all too often excluded from such day-time activities by the attitude of the majority of women—enjoyed being involved with the project.

Once everyone was settled I rather nervously tried to give the background to our position, starting off with the most visible—how we had come by the toys. Then I described the steps already taken, such as contacting the Toy Libraries Association, and from there the actual nature of a toy library. I remember trying to explain what I hoped was to be a group approach to setting up a toy library in our own area, concluding in desperation, 'and now I've reached the point where I can't manage it all by myself'. Not the ideal introduction to a community venture! I was aware of Marg doing her best to 'pull the centre of gravity down group-wards' as I wrote in my notebook afterwards. She was definitely my 'ballast' and yet she kept very much on the side-lines, never dominating the discussion or even directing it.

Half-way through we had a cup of tea and a chance to chat a little before progressing to serious plans for the future. Together we completed an application for a grant to an organisation called Make Children Happy. This led us to discuss a name for the Toy Library since the application required it. By chance we were situated at the junction of three postal districts and electoral wards, so we chose a name related to the main road we bordered. This was our first democratic decision which it was important to abide by even though some felt the word 'community' should have been included. So Burdett Toy Library came into existence. Later in the meeting we agreed to visit the Spitalfields Toy Library, taking advantage of a van owned by one of the group. We discussed opportunities for publicity including local television news programmes; activities which might develop from the Toy Library like organising a baby-sitting circle; an information board; offering things for sale/exchange; and even collecting trading stamps to buy more toys. Next we outlined plans for the exhibition at the clinic. In order to enlarge our toy stock we decided to ask local firms for donations, and to try and collect used toys through schools—although we put off attempting to draft a letter about this until our next meeting. We also decided to invite people from Community Links and the Bow Mission to come soon and talk to us to increase our know-how. Finally, we agreed to meet in two weeks time because of half-term and the bank holiday the following week. I think Marg was afraid that with this delay we would lose momentum.

The next day I wrote to the Toy Libraries Association notifying them of our name—so now we were official. At the same time I asked them to let us have the names of any toy libraries funded by statutory and grant-giving bodies in case we could qualify too, and ordered some of their special Toy Library posters to give our publicity a professional touch. In the afternoon, still buoyed up by the result of our meeting I visited the nearby Pre-School Playgroups Foundation Course and spoke to the group with the aim of recruiting some more people.

At home with a borrowed toy

6 Forming a committee

At our second meeting on June 5th the attendance was not high. Three of the original seven returned with apologies from two others, and two new people came. One was a friend of mine who had been unable to attend the first meeting and the other a local member of Harmony—an organisation I had contacted a few weeks earlier whose members were mainly multi-racial families, some of whom I felt might be interested in our project because of its aims to bridge nationalities (see Appendix 2 (7)).

We discussed our joint visit to Spitalfields Toy Library which had thrown up some interesting questions, such as, whether to charge for toys borrowed and how much; which age group we could best serve on limited funds; if home visits were advisable, particularly to isolated families such as the Asians. We also relayed, to those who had not attended, advice about contacting our local councillors and getting them interested in what we were trying to do. First, we had to discover who in fact they were!

We had three applications for grants in the pipeline now, but had been advised to try another foundation which aided projects in our area and to try the Finance Department at the Town Hall for details of sources of funds available in the Borough. Everyone discussed the broad form the application should take, on the lines suggested by David Moore, though I was delegated to write the letters.

Once we realised that the grant application forms asked for names of committee members we formed ourselves into a committee, at least on paper, to fulfil the application requirements. Later we learned that our group was known as a 'steering committee', formed to bridge the gap before an elected one was created. We initially envisaged rotating the various tasks among ourselves in a democratic way. As time passed we came to recognise each other's particular strengths and weaknesses, likes and dislikes, and decided to abandon the idea in favour of some specialisation which reflected our skills.

We chose Joy as our Treasurer. She was businesslike and even possessed a pocket calculator. Our Chair-Person, Anthea, was calm and diplomatic as well as being a member of a well-known local family which later proved to be extremely useful to us politically. I became Secretary since I always seemed to end up doing the writing jobs anyway. In line with her new post Joy arranged to attend a book-keeping course for groups such as ours held at the centre where Marg was based.

As we continued to discuss our plan to collect used toys through local schools, a scheme emerged to run a Toy Jumble Sale. The idea came partly from fund-raising suggestions in the Toy Libraries Association's leaflet and partly from Jenny who, having lived in the area all her life, told us that jumble sales were always very popular and good publicity into the bargain. At that stage she was the only one who knew how to organise a jumble sale; after several attempts we became quite expert. We learned, for example, that to achieve maximum success it is a good idea to allow two or three months for collection, provide bags for the jumble, and give a clear date when it will be collected. We also found it best to charge an entrance fee and if possible to sell refreshments. Our Christmas Bazaar taught us not to mix cheap jumble with new goods for sale—as the latter only look expensive by comparison and do not sell well.

We hoped to stock the Toy Library with the best toys we received via the Jumble Sale and to use the proceeds from the less good ones to buy new toys. We then planned a collection of toys from local schools. Knowing the importance of personal contact to ensure results, we each agreed to leaflet one school and talk to someone about our project explaining the use we could make of toys no longer required by their pupils.

On a different front we approached local toy firms found in the Yellow Pages. We drafted a letter appealing for donations of toys which would then be displayed at our exhibition together with the name of the donor. We later extended this appeal to toy manufacturers nationally and, surprisingly, received a modest response to our request.

Meanwhile we recognised that our numbers were dangerously low, both for the work-hours needed to achieve what we intended to, and, more importantly, for the need to involve members of the community in these early stages to shape it to their requirements, and to use their particular skills and knowledge to enhance the project. We agreed that we would each contact people we knew and groups such as Tenants' Associations and local churches, to enlist support and reinforce our limited resources.

In spite of the volume of work ahead of us our second meeting ended on a positive note. We felt that something had been achieved and that we could expect to achieve a great deal more. It seemed an appropriate time to invite David Robinson from Community Links to talk to us about the practicalities of fund-raising, publicity and establishing local contacts. We aimed to have as many people as possible present the following week to benefit from his talk.

In the meantime we each busied ourselves with our allotted tasks. Marg researched the addresses of local voluntary groups such as the Rotary Club and the Round Table. Joy uncovered the names of our local councillors at the local public library. We were not so successful in getting to the bottom of the local government bureaucracy, being passed from one department to another in our attempt to get details of potential sources of financial aid. My job involved getting leaflets and a letter-head printed. I eventually succeeded but not without some headaches when the technologies of electric scanner, duplicator and guillotine all seemed to conspire, leaving me with blurred and blotchy sheets of decapitated paper.

7 Casting our net

We learned how to raise funds

To the professional community worker it must have seemed that our development was very lop-sided and far from the ideal, but we were too excited to evaluate it coolly until after we opened and could draw breath. Meanwhile both Marg and Sebastian, in their own ways, were impressing on me the importance of planning one's time well and working to a realistic timetable. I was still tending to rush ahead too fast and this meant I would push myself to do jobs rather than wait until someone else would volunteer or could find the opportunity to help. I had to learn my own limitations for the good of the group because, apart from racing from one end of the Borough to the other and getting hot and bothered, I was becoming resentful over why the others were not willing to join my frenetic pace instead of realising that I was the one out of line.

Our original aim of being open in time for the summer holidays gradually began to seem less urgent. Marg emphasised the idea of building up strong local involvement, stressing that it takes time particularly as contact should be made personally and built up slowly.

One morning Gloria, the Health Visitor, came rushing over from the clinic across the road to say that the Gulbenkian Foundation had phoned her about visiting us. Apparently we had not received a letter they had sent us, so they phoned the clinic mentioned in our application because they needed to know if it would be possible to visit us the next day. As this sunk in I got a bit panicky, what would they think of the room? What, if the committee were present, would they think of us? I was worried that we would appear three middle-class outsiders—not East-Enders at all. In my panic I kept the visit secret from the others but, luckily, Anthea arrived half-way through by chance which at least proved we were a bonafide group! Our visitor Richard Mills, then Deputy Director of the Foundation, was very positive about our project. I was afraid he had read a little bit more into our application than was the truth, assuming that we had done considerably more research into Asian families than we had. Where we had mentioned involving school children, he envisaged those from Asian homes helping on home visits to provide a link between the cultures and languages—which was more than we had! I explained to him the original idea behind the Toy Library—a means of drawing immigrant families to the community house, hoping that then they might meet other local families who could perhaps in turn become involved in offering informal language and literacy classes. It was, I think, the possibilities of this idea that initially attracted the Foundation's attention. Mr Mills' attitude seemed to be positive. He said that in addition the low cost of the project made it appealing, so we were fairly hopeful that our application would be successful.

David Robinson from Community Links came to speak to us at our meeting on 12th June. We asked his advice on how to organise a stall at the local school's summer festival and he suggested that we should aim to use it as a fund-raising opportunity, not just for publicity. He stressed that we should apply for funds from a number of sources. Even if we received our request for £350 from the Gulbenkian Foundation it would not be sufficient. However, on future applications we could quote a larger budget for the project as a whole including contributions already received from other organisations like the Gulbenkian Foundation—which would give us a seal of approval. David also advised us on relations with the media, recommending we supply them with a press release containing all the relevant information about ourselves so that there was less chance of our being misquoted. We could also back this up with photographs of children playing with toys. Another tactic Community Links had found useful was to contact local workshops for the mentally and physically handicapped and any Job Creation Schemes which employed youngsters, to make toys. Apart from this, through the publicity leaflet we could appeal for materials—wood, nails, buttons and so on. In the course of this meeting a newcomer, Thomas, who was temporarily unemployed, offered to make us some wooden toys in his spare time. He had been directed to us by Marg who still kept us in mind. He also offered to put an advertisement in his local church magazine asking for support and toys for us. We were casting our net wider.

Richard Mills from the Gulbenkian Foundation had told us about the intensive Hindi classes that were being organised by Harold Road Centre in Newham to enable English speakers to master basic conversation. Unfortunately we discovered that most of the Asians in our area spoke Bengali; but Marg told us that there were Bengali classes starting the next week at the East End Mission. Three of us started to attend but it proved too difficult for those with toddlers since no crèche was provided. I was able to keep it up since it was in the afternoon when Natalia had her sleep. The following September I enrolled at the Adult Education Institute classes and slowly acquired some basic conversation.

Following David Robinson's advice we made contact with some local workshops. Community Industry, a Job Creation Scheme (see Appendix 2 (17)), made a wide range of toys but I found it hard to judge the quality of the work and the competitiveness of their prices since it was my first experience of buying toys, let alone handmade ones. Fortunately we were offered a good selection at knock-down prices because they were moving premises and also, I think, because they approved of our aim to use the toys in the community. Also on David's advice we went ahead with an application to another source, the Foundation recommended earlier by Spitalfields Toy Library. We discovered in due course that this particular Foundation preferred to make grants direct to the Toy Libraries Association on the basis that they would have the expertise to assess the priorities of each organisation.

Two of these visits I made, to Community Industry and the Harold Road Centre in Newham, caused me to reflect on the project and its aims. Community Industry was a bit disappointing at first. After phoning to arrange a visit I belatedly discovered that I had mistaken the address and unfortunately got caught in a downpour while finding Whitehorse 'Road' instead of 'Lane'. Also I had just bought a buggy for Natalia and found she was unhappy with this new method of transport, not being able to see my face for reassurance.

As we both got wetter and more miserable I wondered to myself whether all this 'Toy Library business' wasn't proving rather a strain on me and her. Although, in general, I considered it definitely worthwhile and even beneficial to the whole family, there were occasional moments of doubt. When things were going smoothly I felt elated and recognised that Natalia was able to have richly varied contacts too. Sometimes, indeed, I found it hard to think back to the days when she and I only knew our next-door neighbours and the route to the shops. This enthusiasm resulting from seeing things moving ahead no doubt stopped my being introverted and depressed too, making me more lively as a person. With each successful encounter my self-confidence seemed to increase and this helped me tackle the next one. The only difficulty was in not trying to do too much at once, or expecting others in the group to do more than they were capable of doing. The fact that I had no job and only one child, neither a tiny baby nor yet of school age, meant that I had far greater freedom than some of the others and fewer commitments. This imbalance among the group may have contributed to the fact that I tended to do most of the time-consuming visits and it was, therefore, an unfortunate result that they often did not share this experience of growing self-esteem and satisfaction to the same degree. In this way a gulf could easily have been created between us where we slipped automatically into the 'leader' and 'follower' roles. Ideally this would not be a risk because there would be a variety of skills in the group—each person developing a particular type of activity in parallel—for the good of the project as a whole.

Joy meanwhile attended the book-keeping classes at our nearby Settlement. As a result we bought a cash box and a cash book in which we entered income and expenditure, breaking these down into toys, equipment, refreshments etc. More seemed unnecessary at this stage but at the end of the year when the man who had been teaching Joy came to audit the books, I think he wished he had been more explicit. We had not differentiated sufficiently clearly between cash and deposit or current account at any given time and, owing to lack of experience, knew nothing of the idea of a petty cash float which would have made life a lot simpler. Our expenses had been fast and furious at the outset. As we did not receive our first income until August we had spent a great deal 'From Jo's pocket', which did not exactly help when it came to balancing the books. There is a useful publication *Basic Book-keeping for Community Groups* which we learned about later (see Appendix 2 (20)).

The toys were respected, and seldom damaged

8 Improving our image

By the time we met again on June 19th we had heard that a Gulbenkian Foundation grant for £350 had been approved. What should have been a time for jubilation at this great breakthrough was instead tinged with gloom over our complete failure to involve the community. It seemed we could hardly even keep our original group going. There were only six of us present at the meeting, including Marg.

Fortunately it was the season for summer fêtes and we had been offered the chance of stalls at two local events. Even though the need for fund-raising was less urgent now, we realised the stalls could provide a good opportunity for drawing wider attention to our plans. At the first one we decided to raffle a large toy and display some of the stock we already had along with information and requests for volunteers to help. At the second we aimed at a small version of the Toy Jumble Sale—selling off toys unsuitable for lending out. Joy's husband, on his own initiative, made us an awning, while Joy and Anthea secretly made a splendid banner to go with it.

At our next meeting on June 26th there were six of us and for the first time we did not have the supportive presence of Marg. We were just beginning to get enough confidence to manage alone, knowing that we could refer to her if necessary. It was an exciting day because the local paper had responded to our phone contact by sending a reporter. She was sympathetic, asked the right questions, and even arranged for a photographer to come right away who took pictures of four of our children playing with some of the larger toys we had bought from Community Industry. The actual one printed showed them staring gloomily at the ground. In the background was an empty cardboard box in which we had carried the toys, prominently featuring the name of a whisky manufacturer. Anyway, it was a beginning, and perhaps would serve to arouse curiosity and draw in more local people since a newspaper article carries a certain glow of importance.

We were beginning to feel rather less optimistic about a real break-through in this area, however, and most of the meeting was spent discussing our image and what we could do to make the Toy Library Project more attractive. We felt we ourselves must be putting up unintentional barriers which were discouraging even the local people who had at one time shown some interest. Unfortunately it seemed that 'like was attracting like' and, unless we could do something to break the vicious circle, we were going to end up catering only for the outsiders living in our area. It seemed we were mainly attracting people who by nationality, marriage, culture or background did not fit easily into the pattern of East-End life.

Such a person was one of our few Asian contacts. She lived on the eighth floor of a nearby tower block. Her English was rather patchy and having come from East Africa was isolated even within the Asian Community, speaking Gujerati rather than Bengali. Another member of the group who joined us at the time, and brought great energy and positive thought to the project, qualified on three counts since she was Swedish, married to a West Indian and had recently moved to London.

Meanwhile we worked hard trying to improve the 'atmosphere' of the room. It was at the front of the house next to the front door leading off a narrow corridor. It measured 15 feet by 27 feet, had a very high ceiling and a fireplace with a gas fire on one wall flanked by two shallow alcoves: all we had were a couple of chairs and two old mattresses placed in the bay window topped by two jumbo cushions to lean on. There was a scruffy nondescript carpet on the floor and the colour scheme—chosen by two fellow residents of the Community House—was dark brown and cream. Luckily the new orange shelves we had put in the alcoves brightened up the room considerably, along with some delightful brightly patterned curtains (which had been made by our latest recruit) and we had enough left over to make a matching cover to go over the mattresses. We also decorated the walls with colourful posters from Oxfam and Unicef (see Appendix 2 (10) and (11)) which featured children from varied cultures and which we hoped would help to make anyone feel welcome and emphasise our multi-cultural approach. In one corner of the room we posted up a large map of the area on which we planned to mark the homes of the people who used the Toy Library as well as amenities in the area like One O'Clock Clubs, Doctors, Nurseries, Playgrounds, Swimming Pools and so on, to help orientate people new to the area.

We tracked down a shop that sold second hand metal shelving and though it was rather rusty and wobbly it looked fine once we had given it a coat of orange paint. We secured it around the door, where it could form the support for a large shelf over the door itself. Here we were at last able to store some of the bulky toys which had been taking up our floor space. At the same time we decided to hang the large fort we had bought from Community Industry on the wall above the community map—which not only looked quite effective but left us more room on the shelves. Space was at a premium and we became quite crafty at finding ways to maximise it. We wanted to keep as much floor space clear as possible for parents to sit and children to play. At the same time the room needed the flexibility to be used as a meeting place by other groups when not being used as a Toy Library. At least its size helped to give it a cosy and inviting atmosphere.

We suffered from lack of space elsewhere. Since it was not safe to leave things outside the house, the passageway got cluttered up with prams and pushchairs which had to be clambered over. The space outside, however, did prove useful after all when we realised it could house a sandpit. We learned from bitter experience that it was better to use silver sand, not the coarser yellow builder's sand which tends to stain clothes. We were advised to cover it at night and disinfect it regularly because it tended to be a favourite with the local cats. We then built a fence around it so that the children could not run out into the road. It was very popular, especially on hot days, except with one little boy who would not go near it because he had seen a spider once and felt unsafe for months afterwards! Its use even helped to attract attention and drew in new members.

As time passed our horizons broadened. As well as constantly improving our stock of toys for the children we became increasingly aware of how we could cater for the parents too, for example, by pooling information. One way we thought we could achieve this was through noticeboards. Alvaro put one over the fireplace which was mainly for local events and advertising things 'wanted' or 'for sale'. Another, in the hall, was for information of wider interest to parents: newspaper cuttings, campaigns and so on. Another method was to collect useful leaflets on topics such as consumer rights, benefits, and health care which we displayed in a rack. Anyone could then refer to them for advice. We got into the habit of collecting likely leaflets from clinics and post offices to improve our stock. We also wrote to bodies such as the Health Education Council and the Family Planning Association (see Appendix 2 (12) and (13)) for any of their free leaflets which we thought would be of interest to parents. On the advice of Philippa at Sunley House Toy Library we wrote to Galt Toys who sent us some good leaflets, and to publishers of children's books who sent us not only mobiles and posters which we used at the exhibition but also a good number of free books.

Once encouraged in this way, we realised that it would be a good idea to have some books on hand to encourage parents to think of reading to their children as well as playing. This led us on to stock a limited range of books for parents too, on topics such as play and development as well as childbirth and health. Originally these books came from our own homes but later we allocated money to buy them when we saw how popular they were becoming. We used the narrow space either side of the bay window to display these, as well as catalogues from toy firms and information from the Toy Libraries Association.

After a few months in operation we realised that we had collected quite a bit of information about our area and, because we found we were always being asked the same questions, we put together a Local Information booklet. It consisted of a transparent folder in which we placed details about under-five provision, Citizens Advice Bureaux, free legal advice and so on. This was a useful addition to the notice-board. Its advantage was that people could just browse through it and find out about things they perhaps had not known existed. Also they could look up problems privately without having to discuss their needs with somebody else. Every time something new cropped up we encouraged people to up-date the folder. Next we built up a similar folder on Further Education for people who wanted ideas of what they might do either with their leisure time or when their children went to school. It contained details of training, refresher and leisure courses at local colleges and adult education classes, complementing the more general leaflets about local events on the noticeboards. One other source of information we supplied for browsing through was a scrapbook called *How Burdett Toy Library Started*. This was partly for newcomers who might be interested and partly to remind ourselves how we had begun and what we had achieved.

9 Some useful publicity

This photograph of the opening day celebrations, October 1979 (by Tony Furby), appeared in the East London Advertiser

The first part of our meeting on 3rd July was taken up with analysing where we had gone wrong with our stall at the Festival the previous weekend and how we could improve in the future. We had found out that the display of toys confused people who quite understandably assumed they were for sale. Perhaps we could restrict ourselves to fund-raising next time backed up by a display board with photos and captions.

Ruefully, we realised that we had barely made a profit on our raffle since the prize had cost us so much. In fact we learnt a great deal from observing the tactics of the stall holders alongside us who were obviously more experienced. One raised a great deal of money with a tombola. It was more successful than ours on two counts: one, because the prizes had all been obtained from local shopkeepers as donations to their organisation; two, that people much preferred the immediacy of knowing there and then if they had won something however small.

One useful side-effect from the day was that it gave us face to face contact with a variety of potential 'users'. Since we had repeatedly been asked the same basic questions about the Toy Library such as cost, age, range and opening times, we decided to print a new leaflet to explain how we operated. We took the opportunity to add an appeal for helpers and useful materials such as ice cream boxes (which could be used to store toys). Meanwhile our meetings revolved around preparations for the opening at the end of the summer holi-days—protecting, labelling and cataloguing the toys and planning the exhibition.

In mid-July I had a phone call from Lesley Moreland, the Director of the Toy Libraries Association, who let us know that our application for a grant to the City Parochial Foundation had been referred back to them. While I was wondering where we would get the additional money we still needed, I heard her say that the Toy Libraries Association would be able to give us the remaining £200 we had asked for out of the money they had just received from Capital Radio's 'Help a London Child' appeal. I could hardly believe my ears, I felt that the Gulbenkian Foundation's £350 had been amazing good fortune and here we were being offered more! It seemed as though we really had no right to accept it. As Lesley Moreland realised, the amount did not prove excessive. There were so many hidden costs apart from the cost of the toys themselves which were becoming increasingly expensive. We wrote to Capital Radio acknowledging their terms and conditions and thanking them. We were able to use the money to pay for items we had not, through lack of experience, even envisaged budgeting for, such as racks for displaying material, the sandpit, a table for signing-out toys and so on.

At long last the ball was beginning to roll. Along with our financial good fortune we found we were also beginning to become known. The Toy Libraries Association, for example, wrote and asked if they could print our letter of application for a grant (which had been re-routed to them) in their magazine *Ark* because it might be of interest to other aspiring toy libraries. Soon afterwards the local hospital radio contacted us and came to tape an interview. We were thrilled to be asked. Four of us were present, each emphasised different aspects of what we were trying to do. As it was a Saturday morning Alvaro was able to be there, symbolising our commitment to the idea that children and play were not just the concern of women. His Peruvian accent also led us on naturally to discuss our wish to reach all sections of the community. This struck a particular chord with our interviewer who was West Indian. He kept in touch with us and often passed on information which he thought might be of use to the Toy-lending Library as he always called us. He also volunteered to come and interview families on the day of the exhibition to help us on our way.

It was as if the project was beginning to generate an energy which, like a magnet, had power to attract people. Perhaps it was merely that we now had more confidence in ourselves. The more we advanced the easier it was for others to see it becoming a reality and feel it worth-while becoming involved.

Marg was still supporting us in her quiet way keeping an eye out for potential helpers or useful contacts. Chance visitors led to unexpected benefits such as an Occupational Therapist who put us in contact with a group of colleagues working with handicapped children who were interested in setting up a link with the Toy Library. Often when I came home I would find someone reading the notice in our front window and would take the opportunity of press-ganging them inside to show them the toys and discuss our aims. One day one of these visitors forcibly insisted on borrowing a toy to which her son had taken a liking. I was certain that we would never see it again and began to have cold feet about the whole idea of lending expensive toys. So many people had told us we would fail and I only had the comfort of counting on the successful experience of other toy libraries. In the end the woman did return the toy and for me that was a baptism of faith: it would all work out.

Among the Toy Libraries Association literature we regularly received as members were details of a course entitled 'Running a Toy Library' to be held in York in October. It seemed an ideal opportunity to gain the expertise we felt we needed: we decided that one of us should attend and report back to the rest. We had just sent off the fee to reserve a place when to my horror I got a phone call asking me if I was prepared to be one of the speakers! They explained that the aim was to refresh the memories of those who had long been in operation and to give confidence to those not yet started. In fact we might easily have collapsed in the intervening months and I would have had a sorry tale to tell in York but fortunately we managed to survive.

Our 'begging' letter to all the toy firms listed in the back of the Toy Libraries Association's *ABC of Toys* (now called *Good Toy Guide*) began to pay off. We had offered to label the toys as being a donation from each company. We received some ex-display stock which was perfectly alright for our purposes. We also struck lucky with an extremely generous jigsaw manufacturer almost on our doorstep who gave us two large floor puzzles as well as many smaller ones for all age ranges. We received a phone call to come and collect them. In my eagerness to carry off our booty I single-handedly carried them home balanced on the handles of the buggy, scarcely able to see over the top.

At our next meeting we fixed the date of the exhibition at the clinic opposite for 7th September. Things were really back in full swing now after a slight lull over the summer holidays. We had a hard core of about ten reliable helpers. Together we sorted out last minute problems such as the paperwork involved in lending the toys. We gave details about the exhibition and our opening to everybody we thought might be professionally interested in toy libraries, under-fives or working with ethnic minorities, hoping they would use us as a local resource. These included schools, doctors, libraries, clinics and community workers. With each letter of invitation to the exhibition we included a poster for them to display and distributed the rest ourselves to our by now familiar shops and 'child frequented' places.

The clinic had kindly let us have the whole room they usually used for play equipment to stage the exhibition. It even had facilities for making tea. Early in the day we started transporting our wares across the road and were soon established there. We displayed our books, leaflets, magazines, catalogues and jigsaws on the higher shelves and put the toys on low tables or on the floor. The local children's librarian supplied about 50 books and publicity material for a parallel display. To broaden the exhibition even further we also invited a member of a neighbouring Borough's community project to set up a stall of toys (many of them home-made) which were particularly suitable for under-two's, complete with pamphlets explaining how to make them. The aim of this was to stimulate parents to consider the potential of play even with very young children. Alongside the toys we displayed a large poster giving details of the times the Toy Library would be open the following week together with names and addresses of those of us involved with the project, hoping to draw people's attention to the fact that we all lived locally. We backed this up with a display of press-cuttings to prove that we really did exist! Outside we had an enormous poster saying, 'Today for one day only—Free Toy Exhibition—come and find out what a Toy Library is'.

The normal users of the clinic came in to see us, also people from the local nursery school, the parks department (who were responsible for local amenities), visitors from other toy libraries and, most importantly, reporters from all three local papers not forgetting our friend from the Hospital Radio. Although the numbers were not as great as we had hoped, we felt we had achieved our aim. Several people had seemed eager to become users and two mothers had offered to help out regularly.

The health visitors were so pleased at the response that they suggested we should be based at the clinic one day a week. At that stage it was out of the question since our prime aim was to keep our image informal, divorced from any institutional or statutory body so as to make it easier for local people to identify with and participate. Some toy libraries, however, do function extremely well within clinics, health centres and so on.

10 Our opening

Open for business

We opened our doors on 14th September. Our first day was quite quiet, 11 families came and borrowed 18 toys and 2 books. Some were people we knew well but there were a few who came independently who had not even attended the exhibition. Some stayed for hours and chatted, particularly about the lack of provision for parents in the area and the difficulty of getting to know neighbours with young children. We asked each new member to mark where they lived on our large wall map so that others could see there was a family with a young child nearby and perhaps make contact. One of the local papers rang to ask how we were getting on and in the afternoon we had a puppet show. That evening we celebrated with a party. At last Burdett Toy Library was alive and functioning.

Things did not change dramatically. There was still a lot of work to be done—preparing and cataloguing toys, dealing with correspondence and exchanging information. We were all quietly pleased to see our efforts bearing fruit. Toys were returned and exchanged, the first practical proof that our system was feasible and workable. As new people joined we tried to give them individual attention and to explain how the Toy Library worked.

Our coming of age was marked by being asked to talk to other groups about our work. We were represented at an Information Exchange organised by Parents Anonymous for all types of groups working with parents and we participated in a group of displays organised by the Urban Theology Unit of the Bow Mission. Then there was my visit to York for the 'Running a Toy Library' conference. My nervousness at having to speak rather fogged my appreciation of the first part of the conference and I was intimidated by the awful listening silence as I spoke. What broke this and helped me relax was the way everybody scribbled down a note about our neighbourhood map showing amenities and members' homes. After that my talk went quite smoothly and I could enjoy the rest of the conference. The atmosphere of warmth and mutual support really impressed me. Roma Lear's workshop on how to make toys from scraps stands out in my memory. I took some of her enthusiasm home with me and we all made some toys with the idea of displaying them for parents to think about making themselves. We began to branch out into another area too. In the back room we opened a 'swap-shop' for children's clothes. People could either bring in some that their children had outgrown and exchange them for others or just buy some for a few pence, the money going into the Toy Library funds. This became very popular and often parents would dump their children in the front room and dash straight through to the swap-shop looking for bargains.

We were by now also lending toys to two local English language courses run by the Adult Education Institute. We had hoped that this would draw the Asian families attending the classes into the Toy Library but unfortunately they turned out to live too far from our catchment area to make it very easy for them to come.

By the end of five weeks we had enrolled a total of 42 families and were well into the swing of things. Four weeks later this number had risen to 53 and by the end of November there were 61. This rate of growth, coupled with more people willing to help on the rota, led to our decision to open twice a week from 10 am until 6 pm Wednesday and from 10 am until 7 pm on Thursday coinciding primarily with clinic opening hours; the later closing time on Thursday allowed working parents to attend.

Toys for the kids, jumble for the mothers

11 Taking stock

As time passed and our numbers continued to swell we became increasingly aware that we were reaching only the tip of the iceberg and that amenities for parents in our part of the Borough were particularly limited. This led to our involvement in a local campaign to convert a disused school into a Community Centre large enough to provide a variety of services under one roof. We ran into problems caused by a lengthy social workers' strike in the Borough which prevented the Council entering the Town Hall and giving their seal of approval to the scheme. This delay in turn meant the Greater London Council were unable to give their support even though we had lobbied our Councillor and received a positive response.

Months passed. The inevitable happened. The building was vandalised, copper and lead were stolen from the roof, the rain poured in. The owners of the property wanted it demolished and would not agree to us repairing the damage. Eventually, despite much work drawing up plans and fund-raising, we had to admit defeat. However, being involved with other community groups and tasting the flavour of politics proved a valuable experience. It not only greatly improved our awareness but made local groups and people holding powerful posts in the Borough more aware of our project and the need for such provision.

Meanwhile life in our little front room was becoming cramped and we began scanning the area for alternative premises. This proved extremely difficult precisely because little provision had been made by the planners for residents to meet. Eventually we found a room within a church hall, right in the middle of the area where most of our members lived. Even though it was up two flights of stairs we felt that being three times the size of our front room compensated for that.

We managed to persuade the parish council that we would be an asset to the building and only then realised that we had not fully thought the move through. We had not made any provision for money to equip and decorate the new premises and all we really owned, apart from the toys, was a set of metal shelves, two wall racks, two tables and a noticeboard. Everything else belonged to the community house. Luckily a number of things were in our favour.

The previous November we had applied for an Urban Aid Grant (see Part II Section 3) which Tower Hamlets Borough Council had supported and duly passed on to the Department of the Environment. The following April we heard that we had been awarded a grant. This was tremendous news especially because it released a lot of our energies used in organising the equivalent of innumerable jumble sales in order to survive and allowed us to plan ahead constructively with continuity guaranteed. The strike had held up payments but when we finally received the back-dated Urban Aid we were allowed to use a portion of it towards decorating the room. Also the Parochial Church Council, our new landlords, kindly cancelled any payment of rent until we had finished preparing our new base. We enlisted the help of young people under Community Service Orders (see Appendix 2 (14)) to do a large part of the painting and general preparatory work. On the whole they worked very well and gradually we turned a large, untidy, scruffy room into a bright and welcoming place. We took advantage of the extra space to provide a seating area for parents to relax and chat, slightly away from the children. We took care to further divide the room into areas of use to make it feel cosier since it was so large and had high ceilings. In the children's area we had a book corner, a dressing-up section, a home play area—like a nursery school in miniature—offering a number of activities which younger children might not get at home as a form of preparation for school. We were incidentally able to put to better use some of the bigger equipment including the wooden cooker and dresser which had been too cumbersome to be lent. Alvaro also made up a shop-cum-puppet theatre out of a set of bookshelves.

We were allowed to use the large church hall which adjoined our room. This became a great asset because it provided additional space for using the larger activity toys and it was ideal for letting off steam and for experimenting with echoes and loud noises. It also provided space for the increasingly popular 'swap-shop' and an indoor sandpit. The next year we introduced yet another use—organising speakers and films for the adults, and special events and parties for the children.

After one year in operation it was time to have our first Annual General Meeting—a legal requirement of our charitable status. We would not only need to elect officers and members to replace our previous steering committee but also present an annual report and the audited accounts. The organisation of such an event rather daunted us but with the support of David Moore it proved a pleasant event which we followed with a picnic.

Writing a report for the meeting caused us to take stock of how far we had come in that year. For a start we still existed, despite the gloomy predictions of many at the beginning. Although we might still think of ourselves as the same group of naive parents who had falteringly started the Toy Library, we had undoubtedly acquired certain new skills and knowledge particularly in finance and community politics. We were even coming to grips with PAYE and National Insurance and the art of duplicating needed to produce our regular newsletter.

Looking back over our well-filled attendance book we saw we had been fulfilling a real need among local families and had drawn from among them a broad-based variety of helpers. Our future seemed on a firm footing thanks to our Urban Aid grant and our new larger and more flexible premises. Our stock of toys and books had nearly doubled. There were other successes which were harder to measure: the satisfaction of seeing a child hugging a long-desired toy, or a tense parent slowly relaxing among friends. Naturally there had been disappointments too, when for instance our trust had been abused and a toy not returned, or the occasions when we had failed to pick up someone's particular need for support and decipher it in time: these all contributed to our process of learning. We, as a small group, were discovering what we could hope to achieve and where our limits lay.

Postscript, November 1981

We have now been in operation for over three years. In many ways little has changed. Apart from a few 'old-timers' our rota of helpers and our members are not the same. Some have moved, others have got jobs, or their children have outgrown the Toy Library. I have handed over the job of Co-ordinator to concentrate on caring for my new son, Orlando. Still the parents keep arriving each week as they hear about us. The cycle continues.

We have begun to have traditions that come with time—such as a Christmas party, our annual summer outing, the stock-taking followed by a grand re-opening in September and so on. Still we take care not to become set in our ways and particularly to make each first-time user feel as welcome as every other who has come before with the option of contributing to our better functioning.

We are still a long way from achieving our goals of a truly multi-cultural centre where neighbours co-operate in a variety of ways. But there are small advances. An Outreach Project is in its infancy, backed by the expertise of the Adult Education Institute's Educational 'Home Visitors' Scheme. We have helped to found a sister Toy Library in the neighbouring ward of Stepney which seems well set on its way. It already has a very different style from ours reflecting the interests of those involved and the needs of the locality.

On a wider front we have begun to have regular meetings with other toy libraries both in our Borough and in Newham; we compare notes and pool resources where possible. We look over shoulders at the flourishing Borough-wide Association in Hackney whose unity has definitely benefited all its members, and hope that one day we may have a similarly successful enterprise.

We continue to learn and adjust to changing circumstances. We have our small crises which very often relate to money, either its threatened end or even its abundance leading to complacency and lack of involvement by volunteers. Between us we try to sort out the difficulties and steer a steady course ahead.

PART TWO
The fruits of experience

1 The practical details of running a toy library

Each toy library varies from the next in the range of people it caters for, whether in age, need or cultural background and will therefore have its own particular atmosphere and style. What follows, it must be emphasised, is not a blueprint for others to copy but merely an attempt to draw together some of the ideas we picked up by visiting other toy libraries, and our own attempts to improve, by trial and error. It should be complemented by the information that the Toy Libraries Association holds regular courses for those interested in learning how to run a toy library. They also have publications which are well worth consulting and they are always willing to help out with any queries (see Appendix 2 (2)).

Choice of toys

When starting from scratch this may seem a daunting task since the field is so immense. However, by consulting existing groups about their most popular and successful buys and referring to the excellent *Good Toy Guide* published by the Toy Libraries Association, this can be made simpler. In selecting our own essential buys there was often a divergence of opinion over whether to provide the popular commercial toys in preference to the simpler more traditional ones. We knew the former were often more expensive, less durable and less educational but we found that to some extent we were bound by what the parents and children expected us to provide. Their choice seemed particularly influenced by advertising on the television or in women's magazines, and at times our consumers seemed blind to other alternatives.

We attempted to provide a balance, with toys designed specifically for co-ordination, discrimination, artistic or verbal expression and similar skills. Usually we found that once an appetite for the commercial toys had been sated both parent and child were willing to consider some of the less familiar ones and perhaps discover their advantages too.

We chose to concentrate on toys for children under seven, hoping to provide a more comprehensive selection by specialising. But we kept any good toys or games suitable for the older age group which were donated to us so that older brothers and sisters were able to borrow a few toys. Our aim was to find toys that were safe, hardwearing and good value for money, while providing some specific benefit to the age range for which they were designed. We learnt through experience not to buy the bigger, heavier toys because they were too cumbersome to borrow for all but the few who had cars or lived just around the corner. Only when we had our new larger premises were we able to capitalise on some of our early mistakes, using them either as a stock of activity toys in the large hall or by creating a home-play area.

My preference was to include a larger selection of home or hand-made toys. This was partly through the direct influence of the work of Roma Lear which had inspired me at the York conference and partly through the ideas of those such as Ivan Illich. By showing toys which could be made and repaired easily I felt we might encourage families to be more creative themselves and less reliant on commercial products.

Books

Our supply started off with simple cloth and board books aimed at encouraging parents to include looking at and discussing them in their children's play. We were often given children's books. If we bought any we tried to specialise in multi-cultural ones to reflect the children's backgrounds as far as possible. Later we began to appreciate the wider advantages of familiarising the child with borrowing books; we hoped it would make the transition to the larger and often awesome public library easier. With this in mind it seemed useful to include some books of interest to parents too; they could then provide a model for the child in taking care of something and returning it. As time passed we built up quite a wide range of books for adults—covering, particularly, areas relevant to parents of under-fives such as child care, health and play, pregnancy and childbirth. This was primarily in response to the type of area we were in where very often parents were not in the habit of visiting a public library or did not have the time to do so but could be introduced to a useful book if it was on hand. We found that simply seeing other parents choosing books either for themselves or their children could help start the ball rolling.

Cataloguing

Toy libraries vary in the degree of complexity they use in cataloguing. All probably have in common a wish to record the details of each toy stocked, when and where bought and how much it cost. In the simplest system we saw each toy was numbered chronologically, including how many pieces it (originally!) comprised, eg 110/12. This information was then filed on its record card.

We followed the Toy Libraries Association categorisation in their publication *The ABC of Toys*, giving a letter to each type, such as *A*ctivity, *B*aby, *C*o-ordination etc. Though we expanded it slightly to include our own special categories such as *H*omeplay, or *M*usical toys. We sometimes got a little bogged down over this—worrying about to which of the equally suitable categories a particular toy belonged— losing sight of the real purpose of the exercise which was to help parents to be aware (by its label) that a certain type of toy could enhance their child's development in a specific area perhaps in a different way from another type. We catalogued our stock in a loose-leaf binder which we subdivided into sections which could be expanded as we bought more toys. We found this more portable than a bulky filing box.

A more complex system involved using two files—one for each toy and another for each child. Then the toys could be cross-referenced to each child's name—partly so that their individual progress could be gauged and partly so that the suitability of a particular toy, according to age or level of handicap, could be assessed. This system is perhaps only necessary when catering for children with specific needs for developmentally suitable toys and equipment.

One useful adjunct to the files which makes the stock more accessible to the parents themselves is an idea we copied from 'The Factory' Toy Library. We called ours 'Which Toy and Why'. It consisted of a large illustrated catalogue featuring the toys we stocked for parents to browse through. We made it by pasting a picture of the toy, usually taken from the box or manufacturer's catalogue, on to thick card. Alongside was a short description giving details of the age range recommended, its possible benefits and varied uses, and any information such as manufacturer's operating instructions. We grouped the toys featured there by age and function wherever possible and hoped that by this means, without being dictatorial, we could convey information about play value and have some influence on the choice of a suitable toy. 'The Factory' also impressed us with its regularly updated list of most popular toys and wall posters depicting toys suitable for various stages of development which served to inform parents in a subtle way.

Labelling

Once the toys are catalogued they need some form of labelling. Here again toy libraries vary. Some label each toy with its own catalogue number, such as B45, as well as the initials of the toy library itself. Usually a permanent marker is used although plastic toys tend to pose problems here. Sometimes letters are scratched on and varnished over.

I felt that the labelling on the toy itself should be as discreet as possible, finding the black letters and numbers disfiguring and over-institutionalising, although they did convey the warning for those liable to be forgetful that the toy must eventually be returned. Some toy libraries found that their proximity to others means the families really need to know from which toy library they have borrowed a toy, though this is rare. If necessary, perhaps the label on the toy bag or box could be more explicit, to make it less necessary to label the toy in such detail.

We found it well worth the effort to label each removable piece separately, for two reasons. One, to keep a toy intact more easily within the Toy Library itself, and two, to notify a parent that it belongs to us if discovered belatedly at home. As time passed we became more aware of the importance of giving parents precise information on how many bits and pieces they were borrowing with each toy to afford them a fair chance to return it intact, so it could be lent out again immediately without having to wait several weeks for parts to be returned.

Preparation and storage of toys

Ideally all wooden toys should be double-varnished using a non-toxic polyurethane varnish. This makes cleaning easier as well as increasing the life of the toy. Jigsaws can also be varnished and, if required, made more manageable for small children by attaching plastic golf tees as little handles for individual pieces. Things likely to tear, such as books or cardboard containers, can be covered with transparent contact film. Alternatively the life of cardboard boxes can be improved by covering them with thick, double-duty polythene. If time permits, wooden trays can be made whose lids can be sealed with velcro to keep the contents intact.

Some toy libraries we visited stored the toys in individual bags made of net with french seams, cords to tie the neck, and a label made of old sheet to identify the contents. This certainly protects the toy and helps to carry it home, but unfortunately some found that all too often the bag did not come back. We found it too inconvenient trying to match toy to bag, since we did not want to leave the toy inside it on the shelves because the toy would not be visible. So, as each family left, we would be rummaging around among piles of bags!

A good alternative for large bulky toys is a string shopping bag so that the contents are still visible. Also storage envelopes can be made out of strong polythene edged with broad colourful adhesive tape, particularly useful for wooden jigsaws or flat games that are better displayed vertically. We also found plastic sweet jars to be useful containers.

Display

This links on to the last section since effective storage entails good display. We found this to be a crucial component to the success of the Toy Library, particularly as we accumulated more toys and choice increased. There are two sides to this question: first, the overall appearance of the toy library needs to be colourful and inviting, preferably with toys neatly and predictably placed according to age and type; second, the display should encourage parents as well as children to consider new, less obvious alternatives.

We found that it was best to use, for as long as possible, the original boxes the toys had been bought in since not only did they have the advantage of giving each borrower the impression that the toy was new, but very often a great deal of thought had gone into making the product look attractive. Also any instructions about how it should be put together, list of contents and so on were automatically included. Once the box becomes shoddy, however, this becomes counter-productive and other containers must be used. Sometimes relevant parts of the box can be salvaged and stuck to the new containers, which ideally should be transparent. Failing this we often used plastic ice-cream boxes since these are hard-wearing and washable.

We learnt that open shelves were the most suitable. Cupboards concealed the toys and the children found them less accessible. Toys for the youngest members were deliberately placed on the lowest shelves within their reach, away from the complex ones, which saved us too much tidying up afterwards! We saw the advantages gained by toy libraries that used low tables for display or imaginative centre pieces to hang the toys from. Similarly, rather than storing jigsaws flat on shelves we found it far better to display them vertically, held in place within their plastic envelopes, either using curtain wire against the back of the shelf or stringing them on a washing line. If space is at a premium these can be rotated regularly to vary the display.

Hygiene

Once the toys are being lent out regularly it becomes important to maintain the sparkling image of the opening day as far as possible.

Incomplete and grubby toys do not make for satisfied customers, and incidentally they are less likely to come back in good condition if there is an air of neglect. Some diligent toy libraries, as each toy returns, soak it in disinfectant for a while before replacing it on the shelves. Probably this is of greater importance when lending to children known to be easily prone to infection. Obviously toys should always be disinfected if it is suspected that they have been in contact with any infectious disease. Apart from the baby toys, we tended to do a thorough clean only sporadically, just wiping over with disinfectant if mucky. Toys made of cloth are far more likely to transmit germs and, apart from this, cuddly toys are not recommended for lending because children become too attached to them. However puppets and dressing-up clothes are possible if they are washable.

Repair

With repairs and making simple toys our aim was always to involve local schools, clubs, workshops for the handicapped and job creation schemes. Occasionally we struck lucky, but in general these plans tended to go wrong. Many toy libraries have managed to build a mutually beneficial working relationship with such organisations. Unemployed or retired people with skills are obvious gold mines. Comparing notes with nearby toy libraries often leads to valuable sources of help.

We always tried to stress to parents the importance of bringing back broken toys because they could often be repaired, or the pieces used to complement 'cannibalised' toys. Lego, pastry and tea sets are particularly useful for patching together once parts go missing.

Charging

Although some toy libraries are free we decided to charge a nominal amount to become a member (30p) and to borrow toys, for two reasons. We felt that paying for the service might help ensure that families valued it more and took a reasonable degree of care. Secondly, we considered it might reduce anxiety about borrowing, by lessening a parent's feeling the need to pay if the toy got damaged or lost since the charge was to cover such eventualities. We, of course, did our best to minimise the problem by choosing sturdy toys and protecting them before lending.

We charged 5p for each toy borrowed, apart from small baby toys which we felt were worth 2 or 3 for 5p. When we found that jigsaws and books were not being borrowed as often as we expected we made them into a special category at 2p each, stressing that as many as desired could be borrowed in addition to the toy. This sales tactic did seem to work and families who had ignored the puzzles began to explore them at last, or considered taking a book.

At first we charged 5p for every toy, even the most expensive ones, so as not to discriminate against poorer families. In time members themselves convinced us that they felt better paying double for these dearer toys.

Non-returners

Despite our novices' fears this did not prove too great a problem, perhaps because the chance to borrow another toy was a very real incentive to bring the old one back, and children do tend to tire of even the most glamorous toy. We often found that there was an excellent reason for delay in returning—a series of illnesses in the family or an unexpected journey. Although we did not charge a fine for overdue toys, some parents felt they wanted to pay extra for keeping a toy too long. For this reason we introduced a Donations Box. For many families the thought of an ever-increasing fine might prevent them coming back at all. Occasionally we discovered that a family had not returned because of anxiety over damage or loss. One of our most expensive and popular toys, for example, was returned after a long absence when a helper reassured the borrower that she would not have to pay for a jigsaw her daughter had tipped over the balcony of the tower block where they lived. This chance to rectify the picture only came when they met at our Jumble Sale since we had failed to make it clear enough when the jigsaw was actually borrowed. If parents insisted on paying towards the replacement of a toy the Donations Box could be a useful compromise.

Nonetheless we tried to be a little cautious, preferring not to let a new, unknown borrower have the most expensive toy the first time. Every so often we came across families with complicated excuses about toys being elsewhere, but with a little persistence on our part they eventually turned up. Our worst experience was to find that a family had disappeared by the time we went to check—the flat empty and boarded up. Sometimes I think they may really have intended to return the toys but at the last minute the chores involved in moving meant they did not have the opportunity to do so.

One of our tactics for encouraging the slow returners was to have a general recall for stock-taking and repair; and if they still did not respond we went to collect the toy without any further ado. It was always important to leave the door open for renewed borrowing once we re-opened, however, by not appearing condemnatory. It was quite difficult to tread the tight-rope between not condoning behaviour that would damage us and yet being fully sympathetic and supportive of families who genuinely found it difficult to organise the successful care and return of toys.

Insurance

We found that toys cannot normally be covered under a house insurance policy. The Toy Libraries Association, however, have arranged a general policy which covers toys in transit and even at exhibitions*. Any organisation employing someone or permitting the public to enter its premises in respect of its employees must, and in respect of the public should, to protect itself against possible claims, take out insurance cover against such people suffering any damage as a result of neglect by the organisation. These insurances known as 'employer liability' and 'public liability' can also be included in the Toy Libraries Association general policy if requested.

Record keeping

Our recording of membership relied on a box file system of cards on which we wrote the name and address of each family, the names and dates of birth of the children and the date they had become members. Our first method of recording lending was to use a Day Book—a spiral note-book—in which the families' choice of toy with catalogue number was written each day. When the toy was returned this date was added and a note about the condition of the toy could be made eg 'one man still missing'.

As we progressed we found the Day Book system rather cumbersome since it meant hunting through the book to discover when the family last visited. Instead, we bought a large attendance book similar to a school register with the names of members down the left-hand side and the dates of opening each week, by column, across the top. As well as making it easier to find a family, through an alphabetical index, it also had the advantage that we could see at a glance if someone had not come for a long time and could arrange a home visit if necessary.

We grouped the names on the register by 'patches'—small territorial areas perhaps defined by a major road, a shopping precinct or a canal which people of each area seldom crossed. In this way we listed together people who were neighbours making it one stage easier for us to introduce them to each other. If this did not occur by chance when they visited on the same day for example, we sometimes achieved it by little ploys such as asking them to deliver a newsletter to a nearby member.

Some toy libraries operate a system similar to a book lending library with each child or family having a ticket into which is placed a card with the date, the numbers of toys borrowed and the return date stamped to remind them when they are overdue. We tended to be less formal and our three-week time limit was intended as a rough guide only, but many toy libraries are more insistent on this.

The role of volunteers

We were advised even before we opened that to serve its purpose a toy library should above all have an informal, welcoming atmosphere. Many parents—particularly those lacking self-confidence—can be put off by the size and formality of the typical local public library so it is important to minimise the institutional image. The emphasis should be on personal contact with helpers present to welcome each family as they arrive. We found from experience that it was useful to have several helpers on duty at the more popular times. Often somebody would come to talk about a problem and choose a particular helper to confide in, or helpers themselves wanted to maintain friendships and chat, so it was important to have 'free-floating' helpers who were available to talk to other borrowers present as well as to deal with the mechanics of lending the toys or answering queries about them.

At toy libraries specifically for handicapped children there is often a qualified professional present to advise parents on toys, behaviour and other general problems. We felt, being a community-based venture, that we wanted to minimise the emphasis on 'the expert' and rather encouraged the users to discuss things among themselves so that their self-confidence as parents could grow. Very often a fellow parent's experience could put a problem into perspective, or practical information could be exchanged over a cup of tea. We realised how valuable this could be when a single-parent father joined, since he rarely had access to these kinds of gatherings and really appreciated them.

For the same reason of boosting self-confidence, we aimed to let parents learn for themselves by trial and error to choose appropriate toys for their children. Occasionally the volunteers could offer suggestions, if directly asked, because of their greater knowledge of the toys available or of ones borrowed by families with similar aged children. Another way a parent-helper could be of benefit to a parent-user was by offering practical help; for instance, we made phone-calls on their behalf to arrange appointments or check facts, if this is what had been bothering them, or we could show them any relevant information we might have accumulated. At the same time we tried to encourage them to feed back anything useful they discovered for the next parent with a similar query so that our pool was constantly enlarged and updated.

It was only gradually that we began to appreciate that the lines between 'helper' and 'user' were beginning to blur. Firstly, our original 'core' group became larger as parents who had come to use the Toy Library offered to help on a regular basis. Secondly, friendships began to expand into the community as families met in the park and so on. We found it extremely important to ensure that users of the Toy Library who did not yet belong to this 'network' did not feel excluded from conversation. Therefore one of the tasks of the volunteer on duty was to introduce everyone present, preferably on a first name basis. Very often a cup of tea would help to break the ice while children played together.

Apart from these social duties, volunteers were relied on to help with all the practical tasks that cropped up. We tried to encourage everyone to choose the area that most suited them. Some painted or varnished, some sewed, others typed. A couple of husbands were highly sought after for carpentry and toy repair skills. We pooled our efforts when it came to fund-raising events.

Selecting volunteers

We did not have a selection procedure as the style of our project and nature of those already involved tended to determine who subsequently joined. Although some toy libraries have a scheme for paying volunteer expenses, we did not, so the new recruit had to be someone willing to help out for the small recompense of free refreshments and borrowing toys for free. We handled money regularly—whether takings for refreshments, borrowing toys or sales from the swap-shop— so it was important that a volunteer should be trustworthy. We tried not to leave the cash box around unattended, and it was extremely rare that anything went missing though we had misgivings about certain users and needed to be on guard.

We found that most volunteers came from a certain group within the community—usually with children coming out of the 'time-consuming' infant stage, and not yet at nursery. They tended to be isolated in some way, perhaps being new to the area or originally from another country, and welcomed the opportunity to contribute to a project which benefited them and their child at the same time. Occasionally someone offered to help us when they were going through a stage of their life when they actually needed considerable help themselves. If so, we tried to pair them with another regular helper and involve them in group decisions as much as possible without putting too much strain on them. Even though at times our own tolerance was severely tested we felt unable to discourage them and had to try to weather the storm together.

As time passed we found that we had a steady turnover of volunteers. Factors such as children reaching school age and parents getting jobs played their part. Something that took us by surprise, however, was the interaction with husbands' expectations and cultural traditions. Perhaps those of us already involved took for granted our family's support and agreement with the aims of the project; this had actually contributed to our becoming 'core' members in the first place.

We found that women who had grown up in a traditional or working-class environment, where sex-roles were most strongly defined, experienced the greatest tension. At the outset things were fine because the benefits to the wife of satisfying her need for companionship and having something to occupy her were obvious. However, if she then became involved at a deeper level—taking work home or helping at a weekend fund-raising event—this impinged on the rest of the family and sometimes the husband became resentful as if unwilling to accept that she should have an interest other than the home. In some cases a compromise was reached, in others the strain was too great and the helper had to drop out. Only by seeing it in this broader context were we able to avoid feeling let down, since by then we had quite a sense of group loyalty. Similarly, we came to appreciate why some women never became helpers at all. Apart from home expectations some had so little self-confidence that they could not risk being proved unacceptable or unreliable by offering a regular commitment. So we would respect their claim of 'not having enough time'.

In fact, we needed to learn our own limits as a group. For many of us this was our first involvement with any such project and we were still discovering our potential. At one time we decided to try to improve our own skills and eventually the service we hoped to offer by linking up with evening training courses offered by Parents Anonymous in the neighbouring Borough. In practice, however, this had to be shelved, partly due to practical problems such as transport, partly due to husbands' concern, and partly due to our own hesitancy at embarking on this challenging course. We felt that we had bitten off more than we could chew, and this in turn gave us insight into the type of volunteer we were actually attracting and could hope to attract to a project of our kind in our area.

* Insurance cover is not automatically conferred by membership of the Toy Libraries Association. For further information, please ask the Association. (see page 67)

2 An approach to Asian families

Our particular Toy Library had started as a means to an end. It was supposed to be the 'bait' by which isolated people were attracted into the Community House so as to meet others in a friendly setting. One spin-off we envisaged was that those in need might then be in a position to request and be offered literacy or language classes by other users—at a neighbourly level. This need was thought to be greatest among the newly arrived immigrant community, who in our area were predominantly Bengali. We were not as successful as we had expected in attracting the Asian community, and in fact the Toy Library took over as an end in itself until the time came when we hoped to have sufficient resources to make this a priority.

From our own experience we can certainly not claim to be experts, but this section may have its uses in outlining the information we gained from those with more knowledge than ourselves, and in highlighting the pitfalls which might be avoided.

Contact

One of the first hurdles we came up against was the basic one of making contact with members of the Asian community. With hindsight we should have devoted far more attention to this at the outset because if we had found even one representative willing to participate in our planning stages it might have smoothed the way for contact later. However, we moved ahead too fast, and relied on chance encounters bearing fruit.

A group more experienced than ourselves recommended tactics such as using the electoral register, specialist shops, centres of worship and so on, as well as referrals by local doctors, health visitors and adult education institutes. Though contact could initially be by an informative leaflet, they stressed it should always be followed up by a personal visit wherever possible.

In some areas neighbourhood English classes already existed but in ours there were none. Though people were employed to work specifically with the Asian community—either by the Adult Education Institute, the Health Service or similar bodies—we discovered that those working in one part of the Borough were not necessarily of any help with contacts in another. In this respect geographical distance was of crucial importance and we soon realised our catchment area needed to be very small if it was to be realistic.

Even drawing out our immediate neighbours raised practical problems—partly because of their cultural patterns but equally due to the very obvious racial tensions in our area which made the women fearful of leaving their homes. Some, for example, had had their saris set on fire, others had been verbally abused. We found that although the men would leave to go to work the women tended to spend most of their time at home, even to the extent of the men doing the shopping and older children doing errands, taking the younger ones to and from school and so on. Because we were aiming primarily at the women, rather than the family as a whole, our task was probably that much harder. On top of this was the fact that the women usually spoke far less English than their menfolk and so had less self-confidence. We realised that any Bengali woman or man who was confident enough to become involved in setting up the Toy Library would have to be the exception, someone who had already made some links with the host community and perhaps had some authority within their own.

One approach I made personally was to the mothers I met attending the clinic. I would explain briefly the aims of the project and judge by their reaction whether they were likely to be interested any way. Occasionally I got a real surprise finding a sari-clad woman who spoke excellent English and had lived most of her life in Britain! In one case a mother did become involved with our steering group, but her husband soon became afraid that by meeting regularly with a group of non-Muslim women she would end up rejecting his values. As a consequence she chose to withdraw from the group. Another casual clinic encounter unexpectedly proved fruitful when a jolly woman speaking fairly good English volunteered to do Bengali translations if needed. When I followed this up it turned out that her husband was the editor of a locally distributed Bengali newspaper which they compiled from their home. Unfortunately her commitments to the paper meant she had no spare time to join our project although she often helped us by placing advertisements in the paper.

Even such powerful channels to gain local publicity did not seem to bear fruit, probably because they were too indirect. Although we put posters in Asian cinemas, shops and places of worship and also had a leaflet printed in Bengali (translated for us by the local Adult Education Institute) we found that response was minimal. Obviously the isolation and suspicion among these families tended to be so much greater than their English counterparts that they would need far more time dedicated to making contact than could be achieved merely by written means. Explanations by word of mouth, preferably by someone of their own nationality, could be far more effective.

Play

We discussed our aims with Greg Smith at the Harold Road Centre in Newham which specialised, among other things, in working with Asians, organising language classes, home tutors and playgroups. He introduced us to further complications which we had not even guessed at and undoubtedly made our task far more problematic than we had dreamed. For example, in many Asian languages there is not a word for 'club' and therefore activities such as Mother and Toddler Club and One O'Clock Club were difficult to understand. He also pointed out that in Asian culture, play as we see it nowadays is given a low priority. Children were expected and encouraged to spend a lot of their time imitating adults—doing domestic chores, attending the mosque and preparing for school by learning the alphabet. When the children had time to play they tended to use natural things like earth, water and sticks. Consequently the idea of a toy library being attractive was rather an illusion simply because having no toys would not be perceived as a lack—unless the parents were conscious of the need to adapt, finding themselves in an urban environment.

In this respect it is interesting to bear in mind that only two generations ago in Britain children would have been quite satisfied with a few simple objects such as a hoop, a box of bricks, soldiers or a doll. Similarly it is only recently that groups such as the Pre-school Playgroups Association have fostered the idea that children brought up in a town need to have their play enriched by including natural elements like sand and water. Considering this it is highly unlikely that isolated Asian parents would appreciate any need for their children to borrow toys unless on the superficial level of enjoying part of the consumer society as portrayed by manufacturers in advertisements.

Home visits

In the experience of those at the Harold Road Centre, Home Visiting (incidentally without toys) had tended to be a failure, primarily because it was unpaid work and as such given a low priority by those involved whose commitment tended to be weak. One old lady, however, had devised a system which had worked reasonably well. This involved introducing a volunteer to one mother, accompanying them long enough for a relationship to be built up, and then encouraging them both to transfer from the home to a centre where social activities and classes were offered.

The outcome of this visit was to make us very pessimistic indeed that our original aims could be achieved. But—if the families will not come to the Toy Library, is it possible that they would like the Toy Library to come to them? This was an approach we found used by Spitalfields Toy Library whom we also visited. It was based in an area heavily populated by Bengalis and set up primarily to serve them. By her own account, the worker who went to the homes found considerable resistance—for example, parents saying they had enough toys. Their policy to overcome this was to take along a selection of toys—including paper and crayons—and the mother would usually be coaxed into letting the children use the toys until the next visit. This at least meant that the children had a variety of toys, although it rarely led to any success in drawing people out of their homes and mixing with others. Since this particular worker spoke only English I wondered how much the lack of communication caused misunderstandings about the purpose of the visit, or failure to pick up on needs. For example, the parents may have been concerned to be saddled with responsibility for expensive toys in case they were broken. This Father Christmas style visit may have been an imposition rather than a blessing at a variety of levels.

Needs of the area

We never resolved this question ourselves and without further research and contact through a member of the community involved— who could interpret or act as the original link person—perhaps it would be impossible to assess the merits and disadvantages. Certainly contacting other groups gave us added insight and by this time we had learned the important lesson that each area has its own needs and style. So, while Spitalfields had a similar ethnic grouping to our own, though far more concentrated, the Harold Road Centre—only a few miles further East—was totally different. Their main Asian ethnic group were Indians speaking Hindi with very dissimilar traditions to the Muslim Bengalis. Fortunately we were pointed in the direction of sources of information on such differences. The Commission for Racial Equality publish a variety of excellent leaflets detailing religious and geographical groupings, explanations of family names and so on. Then there is literature on social and family customs, the effect on these and the extended family of a move to England, and so on. Apart from this we were recommended various texts on language tuition, one of which was called *Meeting Their Needs*, by the Community Relations Commission, although we ourselves never got to the stage of requiring them.

In a sense our original idea of attracting the needy isolated Asian women was turned on its head. Rather than desperately wanting to find ways of joining and emulating their English neighbours, perhaps the Asian women preferred their own company and traditional culture. It was salutory to consider whether our own viewpoint was so culturally biased that we had assumed without question that our interpretation was the only correct one. Perhaps our major lesson learnt was the importance of working with the community as we found it rather than trying to fit a theory onto them in advance. This would apply to any group—whether East Enders, West Indians, or Asians.

3 Financial questions: grant applications and Urban Aid

Grant applications

Since we were so ignorant about applying for grants we consulted a group more experienced than ourselves and were able to absorb some of the rules that led to success. We learned that each grant-giving body may have a different formula for applying and differing priorities favouring certain types of project. There are a few guidelines common to them all which are worth considering:

a.   It helps to be specific not only about what is being requested and how much it will cost, but why, and when it will be required.

b.   It can make your application stronger if you mention other bodies you have applied to successfully—particularly if you have already been granted part towards a certain item or project.

c.   Give the background to your application—how your group developed, how it is managed and what degree of local support you have.

d.   Since many bodies favour funding things which enable a project to continue in the future, rather than a one-off venture, this is worth emphasising, if appropriate.

e.   It is worth doing homework on the nature of the body you are applying to, if possible, so that you do not waste an application unnecessarily.

Below you can see a 'before' and 'after' version of our letter applying to the Calouste Gulbenkian Foundation. In between came not only the realisation that there is a system for applying for money, but that each project has its own need for 'growth'. At the time of writing the first letter, the project was really only 2D, very superficial and thought out on paper rather than based in the real world. David Moore by clarifying this enabled our second letter to reflect a change in approach that had a far better potential. No doubt grant-making bodies are experienced at spotting which projects seem to be correctly orientated and therefore any application needs to have a solid background to be successful.

Here, then, is my original letter (unedited)!

Dear Sir,   April 19th, 1978.

Having read about the Gulbenkian grants for Inner Cities in the magazine 'It's Child Play' I wondered whether you would be interested in hearing of a project we are setting up in Bow (Tower Hamlets). We have the front room of a large house set aside for community use. Seven of us, mostly social workers, are hoping to dedicate our spare time to making the house a welcoming and useful place. I myself have the most free time since I am at home caring for our little daughter. As a starting point we are setting up a Toy Library, specifically aimed at the local Asian community so as to form a bridge with the host population in a pleasant and non-threatening way.

Once we have raised enough money for the basic toy stock and generated publicity we expect involvement to snowball and other related activities to become suitable. One which we are already planning for is an information service regarding local events, resources, agencies and schemes. We have made a noticeboard and are collecting relevant data. Further activities may include language classes, adult literacy and shared leisure activities, baby sitting etc. among the participants.

We feel that there is a lack of this type of provision in the area although the Social Services and other Government agencies have many points of contact at a more formal level.

We look forward to hearing your opinion of this venture and any advice you may care to offer.

Yours sincerely,

Joanna Grana

And here is the information in the form it was actually sent:

Burdett Toy Library: 'Toys Plus' Project Application

Summary
This will be a low-cost community-based project with three aims, all involving people who live within ten minutes' walk of the Toy Library, which is an urban deprived area:
(a) to give young children an opportunity to play with a variety of toys (of the kind their parents would not ordinarily be able or willing to buy) thus aiding their overall development;
(b) to provide a welcoming and informal meeting place for isolated parents;
(c) to make it easier for families from a variety of cultures to meet and make friends in a non-institutional environment (a private house).
There is a group of local women who feel strongly about the out-come of the project and are prepared to dedicate time and skills to it on a continuing basis. A location has been found and a nucleus of toys obtained. We now need a small grant of say £350 for equipment, publicity and related expenses, hoping to be in operation by the summer holidays.

Location
Number 60A Turners Road, E.3. is a Community House leased from the Bow Mission. A large room on the ground floor has been pre-pared for the Toy Library. The Leopold Street Clinic (already a focal point for local mothers) is opposite. The area is characterised by large scale demolition and has a rapid turnover, with the slightly more successful families moving out, while many remain in very poor

conditions waiting to be re-housed. It is in many respects an 'in-between area', much less clearly defined than some others and lacking a social centre.

There are local traditions, firstly of preferring to stay within their own 'patch', and secondly of not visiting their neighbours without a specific reason, which make it necessary to think in terms of a place which mothers can walk to, and which is preferably near some focal point, and non-threatening. Being a private house so near the Leopold Street Clinic, the chosen location seems likely to be a successful one.

First Steps
A small group of local mothers, including an educational psychologist who lives in the Community House and is willing to act as co-ordinator, have done the following:

Firstly research into the area was undertaken to ascertain the response to a future Toy Library. Detailed information on the local population plus existing facilities was obtained. In this way it was recognised that the project would help to meet several pressing needs of the area. Basically it was realised that certain sections of the population had very little understanding of the importance of play to their children, and that the Asian children frequently had no toys of any description at home. Secondly it emerged how socially deprived many of the mothers were. Even among the mothers who had already taken the first step of, say, visiting a One O'Clock Club or enrolling their child in a Playgroup, there was still a tremendous sense of isolation. Many said spontaneously that they had no friends and had no channels for making any. The ones who had recently come to the area frequently found the existing circles difficult to join, and so on. The high proportion of single parent families in the area are in a similar plight.

The Council of Citizens of Tower Hamlets itself has no precise statistics on the proportion of ethnic minorities since the results of a 1975 survey are not yet available, but it is clear, for example, that a large number of the Asian women are culturally isolated and find it difficult to make friends outside their own household, let alone with members of other ethnic groups. They are seen by the European women as an 'unknown quantity'. Given the language barrier and the natural insular tendency of each group there is scarcely any inter-change. It is hoped that the Toy Library by providing 'neutral territory' in an informal setting, joined by their children's play, will make for less barriers.

After the research was completed and the need for such a project ascertained the following steps were taken:

(a)   made contacts with the relevant local bodies, including the clinic, the Social Services, and the Educational Welfare service and also with local schools, nurseries and Playgroups.
(b)   fitted out the room with a small stock of toys, shelves, etc.
(c)   visited other toy libraries
(d)   joined the Toy Libraries Association and obtained appropriate literature
(e)   distributed an initial 500 leaflets in shopping centres, centres used by mothers with young children, private homes and so on, advertising the Toy Library and asking for help of various kinds.

How we will work

We want the project to remain a grass-roots project, responding to a variety of local needs; and we intend it to be out-reaching and flexible, with a minimum of formality. Local volunteers will continue to share the work involved according to their interests, ability and available time. All concerned are committed to the concept of an 'Open House' to which people of all colours and nations can confidently come. It is appreciated that in some cases it will be necessary to visit homes initially to encourage families to use the library. We already have contact with people of some status in the community who are interested in involving the particular ethnic minority they represent. To this end, also, we are already working alongside the inter-racial group 'Harmony'. Apart from the local parents, who cover a wide spectrum, and the four remaining residents of the Community House, who include social workers and a Playgroup leader, we have the active involvement of one community worker and the strong support of another at the local Social Service office.

The Health Visitors at the local Clinic are very positive about the Toy Library and have not only agreed to send clients and publicise it by word of mouth, but are agreeable to our staging an Exhibition within the Clinic. This will be the culmination of our present activities, which are two-pronged. One involves writing to local toy firms, businesses, voluntary groups etc, for donations, either of toys or funds. The other involves contacting all the local schools, nurseries, playgroups and Youth Clubs in a campaign to collect good used toys. This will involve personal visits to enlist the support of staff in each centre plus wide local publicity (press and other media). In the exhibition the toys thus obtained will be on display with a label informing the public by whom it was donated—hopefully an incentive to contribute. At the same time there will be experienced speakers on hand to answer any questions about the purpose of a Toy Library, the advantages of a particular toy on display and so on.

We shall cater primarily for the pre-school age group but siblings and older children thought to be likely to benefit from play experience will not be excluded. Our recruitment will be particularly strong among the ethnic minorities since we feel they are doubly handicapped in an already deprived area, due to their isolation or low exposure to play materials. While the children try out the toys and choose the one they prefer the mothers will be able to have a cup of tea if they wish, browse through literature related to childrearing and play, or review information concerning local events and facilities on a central noticeboard.

The toys available will include the standard ones for co-ordination, discrimination, creative play etc., but emphasis will also be placed on toys which can be made simply and cheaply at home. The potential of everyday materials around the house to be stimulating toys will also be illustrated. In this way it is hoped to minimise dependence on expensive commercial toys, and develop discrimination regarding the function of toys among the clients. The local library is eager to lend books and records through the Toy Library. (Thus parents who may be wary of approaching the Library as an Institution may be introduced to its advantages painlessly.)

We also hope to involve the local secondary schools, should they feel so inclined. Apart from using the talents of the art and craft departments for publicity posters and simple toys/constructional materials, we foresee that the older children who are near school-leaving age would be interested in doing a few hours of community work related to the Toy Library. This could be either by helping during the open sessions (learning about children at play), or home-visiting among the families unable or hesitant to attend.

Regarding legal advice and auditing, this can be obtained free through local centres. Charity status may be applied for directly once a constitution has been drawn up, or for the time being we may merely affiliate ourselves to The Bow Mission, which undertakes community projects and is willing for this to be done.

The Future
We hope it will be possible to hold the Exhibition before the end of

July and to open the Library in time for the summer holidays on a basis of two sessions a week, or more frequently should demand warrant it.

Apart from the basic characteristics mentioned above we expect the Toy Library will in fact provide a springboard for many other activities. Some that we can already envisage as tying in directly are:

(a)   input onto a central noticeboard by the clients themselves, such as events not already posted or advice of objects for sale or wanted

(b)   a co-operative venture to cope with babysitting needs or daytime care of children on a pool-rota basis

(c)   a swap shop for outgrown clothes or similar articles

(d)   a workshop for crafts, toy making and toy repair

(e)   language classes.

If some of these activities become integral to the community and the House therefore becomes a well-known resource we hope other uses may develop:

(a)   a drop-in centre for mothers any time during the week (staffed by a rota of volunteers)

(b)   a centre for meetings affecting the neighbourhood (broader than the territorial scope, say, of a Tenants' Association)

(c)   a quiet spot to come and read

(d)   an advice and information centre for those unfamiliar with the facilities of Tower Hamlets available to them (staffed basically by the residents of the Community House).

Finance

In our favour we have the premises from which to operate and the volunteers (some with related professional qualifications) to deal with all the work of setting up the project and maintaining it, once in existence. We expect to have some response to our campaign for donations, but since it is a deprived area this is unlikely to be very great. A small regular income will be the minimal fee we shall charge for each toy borrowed to pay towards breakage or loss (thus reducing some parents' anxiety over borrowing at the same time). Regarding official sources we have already written to the Commission for Racial Equality's Project Grant Aid plus 'Make Children Happy Trust' requesting aid, but as yet received no reply. We are exploring the possibilities of local government aid also, however this appears unlikely to be forthcoming. The application dates for Urban Aid and the Docklands Scheme have already passed for this financial year.

To buy basic toy stock, prepare it for lending and do related publicity work we are hoping for £350.

Our expenditure is estimated as follows:

		£
Buying basic stock of toys, new		170
Buying locally made toys (jigsaws, constructional, etc)		20
Payment for good second hand toys		30
Stock of Abbatt Homeplay Scheme		25
Preparing toys for lending:	Glue, varnish, brushes	15
	Contact film	12
	Net and tape for individual bags	15
	Paint	7
Repair of damaged toys		15
Posters and balloons		3
Insurance		15
Filing system		3
Publicity and correspondence		20
TOTAL SUM NEEDED		350

This sum would be paid to the Burdett Toy Library Fund.
The Project Group would provide a report at the end of the first phase, once in operation, and at the end of its first year.

JOANNA GRANA, Group Secretary   May, 1978.

Once we were in operation we continued with our local fund-raising/ publicity ventures, particularly in the summer when we could man a stall at annual events. We also kept our ears open for appeals in the media appropriate to under-fives and our type of project.

There are several publications containing useful hints on fund-raising apart from those suggested by the Toy Libraries Association. Grapevine has compiled a useful collection of free information sheets for voluntary and self-help groups. One deals specifically with fund-raising, including relevant publications (see Appendix 2 (19)).

Eventually we reached a stage where we felt we wanted to finance a completely new venture requiring considerably more funds, and for this we referred to the *Directory of Grant-Making Trusts* (see Appendix 2 (21)). In it can be found the details of thousands of bodies which give grants, grouped according to the type of venture they support. A copy can usually be found at a local library but it is important to check that it is the latest edition. By referring to it—a time-consuming but profitable occupation—we discovered nearly 60 organisations to whom we could apply. Though competition is fierce it is always worth trying and even re-applying if at first you do not succeed ....

Urban Aid

The Toy Library was based in what is known as 'an urban deprived area', one designated for the special help of Urban Aid. Since each area has different sources of financial aid, the first step is to discover what these are. Even though we had been unsuccessful in this respect we were rescued by Marg, the community worker, who informed us we were in 'prime aiding season'. We felt nothing would be lost if we applied but had as much expectation of being successful as we had of winning the pools. With hindsight it would have been better if we had done this research more thoroughly because we might have approached it more seriously. Since we were complete novices we made some foolish mistakes. Perhaps their description can contribute to others avoiding them but we recommend always consulting some-one more experienced or the issuing body themselves—in this case the Borough Council.

For a start we worked on the naïve assumption that the more modest the amount we asked for the more likely we would be successful. Although Alvaro argued strongly that it was better to ask for more on the basis that one usually does not get all one asks for, sadly we did not heed him. Apart from that we found with time that we had underestimated the cost of the things we wanted to do, and therefore had to supplement our grant with jumble sales and further applica-tions to sources like Capital Radio's Help a London Child. So, one lesson we learnt was to ask for what we would ideally like, and let those considering the application decide whether it was reasonable or not.

We discovered that it was well worth the effort of doing background research so as to complete the form accurately—for example on the population to be served—since it must convey a better impression to those reviewing the applications. Something else that it is difficult to assess, but may have counted in our favour, is that we sent invitations to all the Councillors connected with the area we served to come to an Open Day at the Toy Library. Here we were able to discuss our aims and they could see what our potential was. In the world of politics the personal connection may swing the balance! Names of local councillors can be obtained from the Public Relations Department in the Town Hall or at the Public Library.

At the time we made the application we had been in operation only a few months, but already we were aware of the need for larger premises and were dreaming of expanding along the lines of Parents Anonymous—providing a comprehensive service for families. We therefore asked for the rent for new premises at what we hoped would be a fitting rate and the rental of an Ansaphone in line with existing groups, but totally forgot the basics like heating and lighting or the cost of equipping and decorating new and larger premises since we had not had to provide for these in our present premises. We only asked for a small sum for toys, plus the cost of duplicating and postage, based on what we had already spent without allowing for inflation or the increased costs of expanding our activities. We thought as far as including the salary of a part-time worker at a 'guesstimate' of £2000 which we conjured out of the air, but forgot to allow for National Insurance, PAYE etc since we hardly knew about them; as a result this had to be deducted from the salary, reducing it considerably. Another mistake which lost us money unnecessarily was that we misunderstood the technical terms used on the application form. We had not picked up that the application was for a five year period and being already confused by the term 'capital' and 'non-capital' expenditure, listed our request for £300 to buy toys under 'non-recurrent non-capital costs'. This meant that we were awarded the money for only one year instead of each year of the grant as we should have been.

Finally when making any application it is best to take a copy before you send it off. We once found ourselves in the embarrassing position of having to ask for a copy of our application before we could reply to the queries we had been asked!

4 Becoming a charity

We discovered that since all grant-giving organisations prefer to safe-guard themselves by making awards to registered charities it is well worth applying to become one. In our early days we were fortunate to be able to receive funds through the Bow Mission, our landlords, who were registered already. In fact any charity can offer to cover a non-registered group in this way if they wish to. Once we realised the Toy Library was going to be a project in its own right we decided to become registered ourselves.

Certainly the simplest way to satisfy the Charities Commission that you fulfil all their requirements is to adopt a constitution that is identical to that of an established charity. Both the Toy Libraries Association and the Pre-School Playgroups Association, for example, offer model constitutions. If queries or problems should arise, Neighbourhood Law Centres can help with free legal advice. We used the Toy Libraries Association's model which at that time mentioned only handicapped children; they now supply a second more general one (see page 91). We followed it closely just altering the first section detailing aims and stating that instead of working specifically with handicapped children we wanted to work with 'all local children under five and their parents, whatever their nationality'. The Commission wrote back querying whether a toy library was entitled to work with parents at all. So we explained how we envisaged our project eventually growing to encompass activities such as language classes and talks for parents. Two months later they wrote back accepting part of our amendment but suggesting we excluded the part mentioning nationality—which apparently they felt to be superfluous.

By this time it was November 1978 and we were becoming deeply involved in a local campaign to convert a disused school into a Community Centre. Others involved in the campaign turned to our Toy Library as being an organisation which could move into the building fairly easily, and if we became a charity, be the legal channel for funding. This proposal caused me hastily to review the terms of our Constitution to see whether we could make such a move. I discovered that there were two serious omissions. Luckily it was not too late to amend our application, so we added two further clauses. One enabled us to pay workers (rather than relying on voluntary help only). The other entitled us to rent or own property. Even though the campaign failed, these amendments were needed when we later expanded to new premises, so including them at the outset saved later referring back to the Charity Commission as is legally required for any changes made to the aims of a constitution.

In early January we reached the stage of being asked for a copy of our accounts—something we did not yet have. As the cash book was practically unintelligible I sent them, instead, copies of the two letters I had written to those giving us grants itemising how we had spent their money. Finally the Charities Commission consulted the Inspector of Taxes and by mid-March we received the coveted piece of paper notifying us that we were a registered charity.

With hindsight, as with so many important steps we took, it would have been easier if we had taken expert advice first. The Constitution needed to include details of the composition of our elected committee, notice given prior to Annual General Meetings, numbers required to make a meeting quorate, etc all of which were far in advance of our stage of development. In our ignorance we had tended to gaily insert figures without a great deal of thought which were later to become rather constricting on the running of the Toy Library;

for example, we began to have second thoughts about charging a membership fee (of 30p) but the Charities Commission by that stage preferred that we leave it in. Similarly our date for auditing accounts ready for the Annual General Meeting was out of line with the financial year, making the picture more confusing once we began to receive Urban Aid annually. Errors, however, can be altered by the membership at an Annual General Meeting, if required, later on.

Toy Library
CONSTITUTION

1. *Name and Affiliation*
   The name of the Toy Library shall be the _____ Toy Library (hereinafter called the Toy Library).

2. *Object*
   The object of the Toy Library shall be to advance the education of local children by the provision of educational and stimulating toys and equipment and in furtherance of such object the Toy Library shall aim:
   i) to assist the development from the earliest age of all local children through all forms of play activity.
   ii) to lend them the best available toys.
   iii) to provide an opportunity for community and professional involvement in a voluntary service for local children.

3. *Membership*
   i) Membership shall be of two kinds:
      a)   User members
      Parents or guardians or minders of all children who use the Toy Library—each family to have one vote and count as one member. Membership is automatic when using the library and paying any borriwing fee, and ceases a year after borrowing has stopped.
      b)   Associate members
      Other interested persons may be invited by the committee on a year to year basis to become Associated Members on payment of such subscription as may be decided by the committee—each family to have one vote and count as one member.
   ii) Members of the Toy Library may attend and vote at

General Meetings.

iii) The General Meeting shall have the power to reject an application for membership.

4. Subscriptions

a) The annual subscription shall be such as may be determined from time to time by the Toy Library in General Meeting.

b) The said subscription shall be due on April 1st.

5. Officers

The Officers of the Toy Library shall consist of the Chairman, Vice-Chairman, Honorary Secretary and Honorary Treasurer. If an officer of the Toy Library or any other member of the Committee ceases to hold office the Committee shall have the power to elect a successor.

6. Patrons and President

Patrons and President may be elected at any General Meeting.

7. Committee—Constitution

The Committee shall consist of:

i) The 4 Officers of the Toy Library.

ii) Not less than 2 or more than 7 additional members.

iii) A maximum of 4 members co-opted by the Committee itself. The President and Patrons may ex-officio attend meetings of the Committee.

8. Committee—Election

Members shall be elected at the Annual General Meeting and be eligible for re-election up to a maximum period of service of three years. Written nominations for the officers and other vacancies shall be required at least seven days before the Annual General Meeting. Provided that no such nominations for a particular vacancy are received nominations made at the Annual General Meeting for the vacancy shall be valid. Consent of all members so nominated will be required.

9. Committee—Powers and Functions

The Committee shall be the governing body of the Toy Library and shall control the management and direction of the affairs of the Toy Library. The Committee shall meet not less than once in each quarter of the year and the minutes of the proceedings thereof shall be taken. At least seven days' notice of each meeting shall be given.

In the case of an emergency the Chairman may authorise the summoning of a meeting at shorter notice than seven days.

A quorum of the Committee shall be 6.

10. *Annual General Meeting*

The Annual General Meeting of the Toy Library shall be held for the following purposes:

a)   To receive and pass the audited accounts of the Toy Library for the financial year ended March 31st last.

b)   To receive and pass the Chairman's report on the work of the Toy Library for the year ended March 31st last.

c)   To elect members of the Committee in accordance with Rule 8 above.

d)   To appoint an independent qualified Auditor.

e)   To transact such other business as may be notified in the circulated agenda for the meeting.

All members of the Toy Library as defined in Section 3, Clause d, shall be entitled to attend and vote.

Notice of the Annual General Meeting and the agenda thereof shall be sent out at least fourteen days before the date of the meeting.

The Quorum for the Annual General Meeting shall not be less than 10 members of the Toy Library.

11. *Extraordinary General Meeting*

An extraordinary General Meeting of the Toy Library may be summoned at any time by the Chairman of the Toy Library or not less than 10 members (or one-fifth of the Toy Library membership, whichever is the lesser number) of the Toy Library meeting together, who shall send a written request to the Hon. Secretary of the Toy Library to convene such a meeting. The request shall be laid before the Chairman of the Toy Library who shall authorise holdings of the Extraordinary General Meeting within twenty-eight days of the receipt of the request. The business of the meeting shall be set out in the notice of the meeting. At least fourteen days' notice shall be given of an Extraordinary General Meeting. Where, however, in the judgement of the Officers of the Toy Library an emergency has arisen demanding immediate meeting, the notice shall be such as they, in the circumstances, deem to be sufficient.

12. *Voting at Meetings*
Voting at meetings shall be by show of hands, but the Chairman may, at his discretion, direct a ballot to be taken, and shall so direct if requested to do so by one-third of the members present.

13. *Accounts*
   a) Proper books shall be kept by the Hon. Treasurer showing:
      i) All monies received and expended by the Toy Library
      ii) All assets and liabilities of the Toy Library.
   b) All cheques shall be signed by two out of any five named signatories appointed by the Committee, one of whom shall normally be the Treasurer.
   c) The Hon. Treasurer shall give financial report at each committee meeting and shall submit a statement of accounts if the Chairman asks for it.
   d) At the end of the financial year the Treasurer shall prepare accounts which after audit by an independent auditor appointed by the committee, shall be presented to the Annual General meeting.
   e) The funds of the library shall only be used for the purposes of the library and no payment shall be made to any member except
      i) if that member is employed by the Toy Library
      ii) If that member is in receipt of an honorarium approved by the General Meeting of the Toy Library
      iii) as repayment of expenses properly incurred on behalf of the Toy Library
      iv) as interest at a reasonable rate on money lent to the Toy Library.

14. *Alterations to Constitution*
No alterations may be made to this Constitution without the same having been duly resolved by a majority of not less than three-quarters of members present at a General Meeting of the Toy Library and in cases where it is desired to amend or add to the object of the Toy Library (Clause 2) without subsequent final consent being obtained from the Charity Commission.

15. *Dissolution of the Toy Library*

If as instructed by a resolution of three-fourths of the members attending and voting at a General Meeting, the committee shall arrange for the Toy Library to be dissolved and any remaining funds or equipment shall be transferred to another charitable local organisation having similar objects or to the Toy Libraries Association. If there is no Annual General Meeting for two successive years, and if no member of the committee makes the necessary arrangements, any other member may do so.

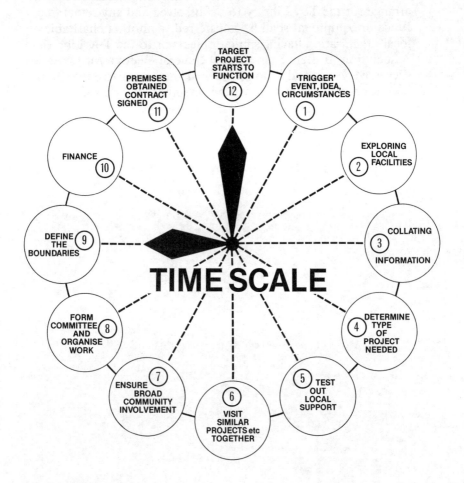

TARGET
PROJECT
STARTS TO
FUNCTION
12

'TRIGGER'
EVENT, IDEA,
CIRCUMSTANCES
1

PREMISES
OBTAINED
CONTRACT
SIGNED
11

EXPLORING
LOCAL
FACILITIES
2

FINANCE
10

COLLATING
3
INFORMATION

DEFINE
THE
9
BOUNDARIES

DETERMINE
4 TYPE
OF
PROJECT
NEEDED

FORM
COMMITTEE
AND
8
ORGANISE
WORK

5 TEST
OUT
LOCAL
SUPPORT

ENSURE
7
BROAD
COMMUNITY
INVOLVEMENT

6
VISIT
SIMILAR
PROJECTS etc
TOGETHER

TIME SCALE

APPENDICES

APPENDICES

1 A possible route to follow

This is meant to serve as a summary of the route we ourselves took (with a few of the wrinkles ironed out and a lot of hindsight). The diagram Time Scale shows the essence of it (see page 96).

A   Once you have the urge to start:
    Explore local facilities existing in your community and use
    them to get as much information on resources as possible:
    eg — Library and Citizens Advice Bureau, for addresses of local
         groups, clubs etc.
       — Clinics (health visitors can be goldmines for contacting the
         right people).
       — Social Services—is there a Community Liaison Officer?
         (can be a source of advice on legal requirements).

B   Try to become aware of which services your area lacks and
    hence which sort of project would be appropriate. Once this has
    been narrowed down:
       — Test out local support, unless there is already a strong
         feeling locally about a certain issue.
       — Seek publicity by word of mouth, leaflets, posters in places
         where the necessary section of the community will see
         them. Then try calling a meeting. If appropriate form a
         steering committee.

C   Hopefully arrange for the majority present to go on to the next
    stage together:
    eg — Visit similar projects, contact any central body that can
         supply relevant information, like the Toy Libraries
         Association.
    Don't be afraid to show your ignorance or naivety and keep
    asking until you are satisfied you have the information you
    need.

D   Do your best to ensure broad community involvement. Although
    this may take time and effort, in the long term it is worth it, to

keep the work evenly spread and maximise support so the project won't be just a brief flash in the pan or incorrectly orientated.

Analyse where the main areas of work are and organise who will be in charge of them.

Ensure good communication and feedback among all those involved. Try to develop the art of making everyone who has shown interest feel a worthwhile participant. Especially avoid an élite group forming.

E   Define the boundaries:
eg – Whom will the project serve and when?
    – What are the costs involved?
    – What are the day-to-day requirements, such as volunteers on a rota, minimum equipment?

F   Finances need researching. Check out all kinds of fund-raising possibilities:
eg – The Directory of Grant-Making Trusts.
    – Local Government funding (Urban Aid etc).
    – Special local funds, events at which to participate.
    – DIY events—jumbles, sponsored events.
Also get expert advice on book-keeping. Open bank account. Contact Charities Commission if relevant.

G   Assuming you have the finances and people power, settle details of premises, contracts etc. Aim for wide publicity at the opening.

2 Some useful addresses and hints

1. Newham Parents Centre
   747 Barking Road
   Plaistow
   London E13 9ER
   Telephone: 01-472 2000
   Contact: Mrs Jean Taylor
   This style of community-orientated project run by local people
   is well worth contacting for advice before you even start.

2. The Toy Libraries Association
   Seabrook House
   Wyllyotts Manor
   Darkes Lane
   Potters Bar
   Herts EN6 2HL
   Telephone: 0707 44571
   Contact: Mrs Lesley Moreland (Director)
   Absolutely essential for practical and emotional support, maybe
   even financial! Lots of useful literature, especially their *Good
   Toy Guide* which includes names and addresses of toy manu-
   facturers and suppliers.
   They can also put you in touch with existing toy libraries of
   many varieties, whether run with funding from the Social
   Services, Health or Education Authorities, in conjunction with
   Public Libraries or run by volunteers.

3. Pre-School Playgroups Association (Main Office)
   Alford House
   Aveline Street
   London SE11 5DH
   Telephone: 01-582 8871
   Lots of useful literature applicable to all sorts of projects that
   deal with parents and under-fives. There may be a training
   course nearby whose tutors may be willing to advise on prob-
   lems related to play, types of toys, local stockists and so on.

Their experience with involving parents is highly relevant, eg *Report on Parental Involvement in Playgroups*, published by PPA, 1980. Cost £1.00.

See also *Grants and How to Apply for Them*, cost 25p.

4. Cope
    19-29 Woburn Place
    London WC1H 0LY
    Telephone: 01-278 7048
    Contact: Mary Willis
    Specialises in preventative work with families and aspects such as involvement, group dynamics etc.

5. OPUS (Organisation for Parents Under Stress)
    National Coordinating Committee of Self-Help Groups for Parents Under Stress
    Mrs Caroline Baisden (Chairwoman)
    29 Newmarket Way
    Hornchurch RM12 6DR
    Telephone: 49 51538
    Contact: Margaret Turner (1981/2). Telephone: 0729 38010
    Fairly new but high-powered body concentrating on parental self-help relating to problems ranging from baby-battering to incest. On the lines of Parents Anonymous but includes a variety of groups all over the country. They produce excellent information sheets and a regular newsletter. Can advise on all kinds of problems and can suggest other organisations specialising in problems faced by parents.

6. VOLCUF (Voluntary Organisations Liaison Council for Under-Fives)
    11 South Hill Park
    London NW3 2ST
    Telephone: 01-435 0082
    Contact: Elsa Dicks (Home)
    Their aims are "to share resources, information and improve quality of care and parental choice". Their knowledge and experience is formidable. Run occasional seminars and conferences.

7. 'Harmony'
   42 Beech Drive
   Boreham Wood
   Herts WD6 4QU
   Telephone: 01-952 8862
   Contact: Carol Carnal (Coordinator)
   An informal and supportive organisation for multi-cultural
   people, particularly couples of mixed marriages and adoptive
   parents of black and mixed race children. Can advise on a
   myriad of things such as multi-cultural books and toys. Social
   events and workshops regularly organised.

8. Commission for Racial Equality (National)
   Elliot House
   Allington Street
   London SW1E 5EH
   Telephone: 01-828 7022
   Local Contact: Community Relations Council
   Useful for varied literature relating to all aspects of ethnic
   minorities culture, contact addresses etc. Possible financial
   support. (See also 9, 10, and 11.)

9. The Commonwealth Institute
   Kensington High Street
   London W8 6NQ
   Telephone: 01-603 4535
   As above, also produce literature on dress, food etc. Have items
   for sale or loan.

10. Oxfam (Head Office)
    274 Banbury Road
    Oxford OX2 7DZ
    Telephone: Oxford 56777
    also:
    Ujamaa Education Department Centre
    14 Brixton Road
    London SW9 49Y
    Telephone: 01-582 2068

and in North London:
Archway Development and Education Centre
173 Archway Road
London N6 5BL
Telephone: 01-348 3030
Useful for leaflets, posters, multi-cultural information. Items for sale or loan.

11. UNICEF (United Kingdom)
    46 Osnaburgh Street
    London NW1 3PU
    Telephone: 01-388 7487
    or:
    84 Broomfield Place
    Chelmsford CM1 1FS
    Essex
    Telephone: 0245 84622
    Good for leaflets and posters.

12. Health Education Council
    78 New Oxford Street
    London WC1A 1AH
    Telephone: 01-637 1881

13. Family Planning Association (Head Office)
    27 Mortimer Street
    London W1N 7RJ
    Telephone: 01-636 7866
    Both the above useful sources for leaflets of interest to parents.
    Similarly Social Security Offices, Post Offices, Clinics etc.

14. Community Service Centre
    480a Holloway Road
    London N7 6HT
    Telephone: 01-263 4357
    Contact local probation department for information on your own area. These centres organise community service orders imposed by courts. The maximum number of hours per week per person is 12, minimum 6.
    Any workers connected with this scheme are likely to be relatively short term and this can cause problems of discontinuity.

However, other problems such as non-attendance or behaviour are dealt with by the probation officer concerned with each individual. Projects such as weekend painting can sometimes be supervised by a paid worker from the Centre, if numbers warrant it.

15. Community Service Volunteers
    237 Pentonville Road
    London N1 9NJ
    Telephone: 01-278 6601
    This organisation involves young people in full-time community service for 4-12 months usually away from their home area. Project is responsible for providing the volunteer with board, lodging, pocket money and travelling expenses.

16. Council for Voluntary Service (London)
    c/o London Voluntary Service Council (CVS Department)
    68 Chalton Street
    London NW1 1JR
    Telephone: 01-388 0241
    This exists in many areas of the country and serves as an umbrella group for a wide range of local voluntary organisations in an advisory capacity and also as a means of contact between potential volunteers and voluntary groups.
    They have a wide range of publications and specialise in providing information, training and general advisory services for voluntary organisations.
    Outside London contact:
    National Council of Voluntary Organisations
    26 Bedford Square
    London WC1 3HU
    Telephone: 01-636 4066

17. Community Industry (Central Office)
    14 Stratford Place
    London W1N 9AF
    Telephone: 01-408 0424
    A Job Creation Scheme for school leavers. It only operates in certain parts of the country. Can be useful for toy making and repair.

18. The Charity Commission
    14 Ryder Street
    London SW1Y 6AH
    Telephone: 01-214 6000

19. Grapevine, BBC Television
    London W12 8QT
    Publish an excellent series of information sheets of use to self-help schemes. Send a s.a.e. for their list of those available.

20. *Basic Book-Keeping for Community Groups*, by Jim Smith.
    Published by Community Work Service. Available price 65p from London Voluntary Service Council address as in 16 above.

21. *Directory of Grant-Making Trusts*, price in 1981 £32.50, published by
    The Charities Aid Foundation
    48 Pembury Road
    Tonbridge
    Kent TN9 2JD
    Telephone: 0732 356323